HOW TO IDENTIFY SUICIDAL PEOPLE

A SYSTEMATIC APPROACH TO RISK ASSESSMENT

Thomas W. White, PhD

The Charles Press, Publishers
Philadelphia

The Charles Press, Publishers
Post Office Box 15715
Philadelphia, PA 19103

(215) 545-8933 Telephone
(215) 545-8937 Telefax
mailbox@charlespresspub.com
http://www.charlespresspub.com

Library of Congress Cataloging-in-Publication Data

White, Thomas W.
How to identify suicidal people:
a systematic approach to risk assessment
p.   cm.
Includes bibliographical references and index
ISBN 0-914783-83-1 (alk. paper)
1. Suicidal behavior — Diagnosis. 2. Suicidal behavior — Patients —
Psychological testing. 3. Suicidal behavior— Prevention.
I. Title.
RC569.W478 1999
616.85'8445075 — dc21
97-33403

Printed in the United States of America

ISBN 0-914783-83-1

Acknowledgments

I wish to thank my friend and colleague, Dr. Dennis J. Schimmel, whose depth of knowledge, insightful comments and editorial suggestions were invaluable in writing this book.

Most importantly, I want to express my special gratitude to my wife, Phyllis, without whose encouragement and never-ending support this book could not have been written.

Disclaimer

The guidelines presented in this book should not be considered a standard of care. Standards of medical care must be determined on the basis of all clinical data available for each individual case and are subject to change as scientific knowledge and technology advances and patterns evolve. The assessment system presented in this book should be considered only as a guideline. Adherence to it will not ensure a successful outcome in every case, nor should it be construed as including all proper methods of assessment or excluding other acceptable assessment methods. The ultimate judgment of risk for suicide concerning each individual patient must be made by the practitioner based on the clinical data presented by the client and on available information regarding that client. Furthermore, the material presented in this book is based on the private views and opinions of the author and should not be construed as reflecting the views of the U.S. Department of Justice or the Federal Bureau of Prisons.

Contents

Preface

The suicide assessment system presented in this book was born of practical necessity and nurtured over almost 25 years of professional experience as a psychologist in the Federal Bureau of Prisons. During that time, I was a practicing clinician, a supervisor and an administrator of the psychology program. With each of these roles, I gained a new and deeper awareness of the dire need for a comprehensive system that practitioners could use to assess suicidality. Each role influenced my thinking about effective methods of conducting suicide assessments and ultimately, each contributed to the system that I have presented here.

Perhaps no experience was more influential in the development of this system than the fact that I too at one time had to learn how to conduct suicide assessments. I will never forget the first time I was asked to evaluate a potentially suicidal client. It didn't take me long to realize that I really wasn't sure how to approach the assessment. I didn't know what to do, what to look for or what to ask the client. This was an extremely sobering experience, especially in light of the seriousness of the task at hand. It was obvious that the hours of theory, research and supervision I received during my clinical training, although very important, had not really prepared me to conduct a suicide assessment with any kind of confidence or self-assurance. Ultimately, the client and I survived, but this was due mostly to a mixture of common sense and a measure of good fortune. Later it became clear to me that what was lacking from my graduate training was a clinically applicable set of guidelines that would help me to recognize the factors that are necessary for identifying suicidal people and to organize and structure the assessments. The material presented in this book is the end product of my personal search for an effective method of conducting suicide assessments.

Today, after years of trial and error, I have a better grasp of the clinical and practical issues involved in suicide assessment. I have also been able to use what I have learned in clinical practice to supervise and train others. From this experience, I know that many new clinicians feel the same kind of uncertainty and apprehension about conducting suicide assessments that I felt when I started out. Despite having had some of the best training available, many of the new psychologists I encounter are still unprepared to conduct even adequate suicide assessments. Throughout their years of academic training, they were given little assistance and basically left to their own devices to discover methods of assessing risk. In light of the importance of conducting accurate assessments, this hit-or-miss system is highly problematic and needs to be seriously re-evaluated. It is not sufficient for this change to occur in one clinician at a time. In the interests of promoting a broader and more meaningful change, it is my hope that this book will stimulate creative thought throughout the entire mental health community by bringing consistency to clinical training and a measure of quality control to clinical practice.

Today, as a program administrator responsible for the coordination and oversight of suicide prevention programs, I view suicide assessment from an entirely different perspective.

These duties have made me appreciate the impact of the legal process on those who provide clinical services involving suicide. Over the years, I have watched the courts play an ever-expanding role as the final arbitrator of disputes about the adequacy of suicide assessments. In today's legalistic environment, any evaluation of risk can ultimately find its way into the courtroom, and once there, it will be evaluated by the rules and criteria of the legal system, not the mental health system. This fact has only increased my understanding of the importance of conducting suicide assessments that are not only clinically relevant, but legally defensible as well. For this reason, this book makes a deliberate point of merging the clinical and legal aspects of the assessment process. My goal in taking this approach is not to coach clinicians on how to avoid lawsuits, but to enable them to conduct assessments that are clinically valuable and legally defensible. By accomplishing both of these tasks simultaneously, clinicians will be able to balance their need to provide high-quality care with a reasonable measure of protection from unfounded litigation.

Notes on the Text

Readers should be aware of a number of important organizational and stylistic decisions I made while writing this book. First, let me address the content. In an effort to concentrate on the underdeveloped and highly underserved subject of suicide assessment, I have chosen not to deal with the important subject of treatment. I'll be the first to admit that separating the task of assessing clients from the task of treating them is in many ways an artificial distinction because, technically, the two go hand in hand. Suicide assessments are conducted in order to determine treatment. Furthermore, in most cases, the practitioners who conduct suicide assessments also develop the treatment plans. The treatment of suicidal people is a complex and detailed subject that deserves a book of its own

— and it is, in fact, covered in a great many of them. However, my concern in this book is to help practitioners with the practicalities and difficulties of the assessment itself, a need that, in my opinion, has not yet been met. To do this, I have had to restrict myself from dealing with treatment issues.

Second, the organization of the chapters requires some explanation. This book provides the reader with a detailed system for conducting suicide assessments that draws upon many coexistent elements. Because each element of the system is presented sequentially in a separate chapter, it suggests that the assessment should be conducted in a step-by-step fashion, starting with the first step and proceeding to the last. In fact, this is not the case. The components of this assessment system are probably best understood as existing in a circle, where there is no single starting or ending point. I have presented the steps in this linear sequence because it seemed to be the only way to present the material in a written format. Moreover, depending on the particular characteristics of each case and client, practitioners may find that it makes more sense to collect data on the client in a different sequence. For example, when you have a client who has an involved psychiatric history, you may choose to address psychological factors first. When you have a client who recently attempted suicide, you may choose to start by addressing issues relating to lethality. Ultimately, far more important than following a particular sequence when gathering information is making sure that each variable is indeed examined during the assessment and reported in the documentation. In fact, these data may be obtained in any sequence, even simultaneously, throughout the assessment process.

I have also made a number of stylistic decisions about the terms used to describe both suicidal people and service providers. These decisions were made to simplify the writing process and make the text easier to read. I have, for example, used masculine pronouns throughout the book. This is not intended to reflect or imply any gender bias. I chose the traditional style of reference only to avoid clumsiness and confusion for the reader. Similarly, I chose to use the word "client" to describe those being evaluated during the assessment process. Depending on the setting, the most applicable term may be patient, resident, inmate or student, but the term client seems to be the least restrictive way to think about the person being served. Also, I usually refer to those conducting the assessment as "clinicians" or "practitioners" even though I have written the book for a wide range of service providers, including doctors, nurses, psychologists, psychiatrists, police and correctional officers, chaplains, counselors, therapists and teachers. I hope readers will find that the use of these terms is sufficiently comprehensive to encompass their particular professional disciplines.

Thomas W. White, PhD

CHAPTER 1

Suicide Risk Assessment: The Central Issues

Thirty-two thousand people in the United States will commit suicide this year. Nine times that many people will try to kill themselves. While some people truly wish to end their own lives, the overwhelming majority of those who attempt and/or complete suicide do not want to die as much as they want to end a devastatingly painful situation. In other words, if they could find a way to solve or end their problems other than through suicide, they would most likely choose to go on living. The key to helping these people is identifying them before they kill themselves.

Unfortunately, this is not an easy task because there is still a great deal that we don't know about the factors that influence people to commit suicide or how those factors come together at a particular point in time to trigger the suicidal act. Adding to this problem is the fact that suicide is a relatively rare act, so we don't have a large sample of people whose suicides can be studied. To make matters worse, the people who can provide the best information about why people kill themselves are dead. As a result, most of the research about suicide is based on retrospective data from interviews with people who knew or interacted with the deceased. There are many problems with getting information from these kinds of informants. They may not know about important events in the suicide's life and their reports may be biased, misinformed or simply wrong. The other way we can obtain information about people who commit suicide is by studying the group that most resembles them — suicide attempters. There are many methodological problems with using this group, the most important of which is that people who attempt suicide may be very different from those who complete suicide. In the end we are left with very limited information about the factors that lead people to suicide and poor predictive measures to determine who will commit suicide.

SUICIDE: AN OCCUPATIONAL HAZARD

The suicide of a patient or a client is one of the most dreaded outcomes of clinical work; the effects can be devastating, both professionally and emotionally. As one national study reported, when clinicians lose patients to suicide, or even when a patient attempts suicide, they react in much the way they would to the death of a family member, with feelings of loss, anger, guilt and helplessness (Chemtob et al., 1988).

Perhaps no role is more stressful than that of the clinicians who are responsible for assessing a client's risk for suicide. It is their responsibility to evaluate clients and determine what the chances are that they will kill themselves. While no one can actually predict whether a person will kill himself — we can only determine where a person lies on the continuum of risk at a given point in time — if a clinician is wrong in his assessment of risk, a patient may die. In fact, evaluating individuals for suicide risk is one of the few occasions when mental health providers have to make decisions that can have immediate life-or-death consequences. In a definite understatement, one researcher commented that "the management of suicidal patients may be a higher risk professional endeavor than most other clinical situations" (Bongar, 1993).

Contrary to what many people think, client/patient suicide is not a rare event in the careers of mental health professionals. Recent empirical findings show that the average psychologist who works directly with patients has more than a 1 in 5 chance of suffering the blow of patient suicide. For psychiatrists, there is a startling 50 percent chance that a patient will commit suicide (Bongar, 1993), and even for psychiatric residents, patient suicide has been described as a "common, if not universal part" of their residency (Henn, 1978). Another study reported that psychologists in graduate clinical programs have a 1 in 7 chance of encountering a suicide during their training (Brown, 1987). As one group of researchers summed it up: "it is not a matter of whether one [of their patients] will someday commit suicide but of *when*" (Fremouw et al., 1990). The time has come "to outwardly acknowledge patient suicide as an important occupational hazard" (Chemtob et al., 1989).

LACK OF STANDARDS AND GUIDELINES

To further complicate matters, today in the United States, we have no accepted and established national standards of care that provide practitioners with clear direction on what constitutes adequate care. And despite this need, there have been few serious efforts by professional organizations and institutions of higher education to develop techniques that would improve our ability to identify and assist those who are suicidal. Professional groups are hesitant to establish specific standards and guidelines for suicide assessment (and for other similar clinical tasks) partly because they are afraid that it would infringe on and restrict practitioners' freedom to exercise their personal clinical judgment and to be innovative when they are treating clients. Another reason for this hesitance to set standards stems from the resistance by medical malpractice defense lawyers who argue that it is much more difficult to defend practitioners who violate an explicit standard of care. While these attempts to protect practitioners are laudable, terrible confusion and problems have arisen because legal standards have been developed but there are no corresponding mental health standards.

With no accepted standards or guidelines, the criteria for performing suicide assessments are left to the discretion of each individual practitioner or, in legally disputed cases, to the courts. One problem with legally disputed suicide cases is that even though there are legal standards (e.g., providing a minimum standard of care), expert witnesses and attorneys can argue for "standards" of their own. For example, an expert witness may insist that an assessment was substandard because the practitioner did not use a particular procedure that the witness claims is "essential." Without professionally accepted standards of care to serve as guidelines, the judge or jury may take the expert's word that the procedure was indeed "essential." To make matters worse, both sides use their own expert witnesses who seldom agree with each other. Inconsistent at best and chaotic at worst, for the practitioner being sued, this legal process is like having a root canal without anesthetic.

LACK OF EDUCATION AND TRAINING

Compounding the problem is the fact that practical training in suicide assessment and management in most graduate programs is limited, and what little there is is terribly inadequate (Bongar and Harmatz, 1989; Bongar, 1992). Less than a decade ago, it was reported that only 35 percent of graduate programs in clinical psychology offered any formal training in the study of suicide (Bongar and Harmatz, 1989), and the situation is probably even worse today. This is also true for the other core mental health professions. One study reported that there is little routine formal training in psychiatric residency and nursing programs and schools of social work (Berman, 1986). Furthermore, a more recent study has shown that formal training in suicide is offered in only one half of the accredited undergraduate nursing programs (Bongar, 1993).

My own experience with new graduates is that even after many years of higher education, followed by internship or practicum experiences, they still seem minimally prepared for assessing suicidality — probably the most important clinical decision they will be asked to make. Of added concern is that most graduate programs seem to pay little or no attention to risk management, putting students and new graduates at a distinct disadvantage when it comes to conducting legally safe suicide assessments. Not only is graduate training limited, but it can also be difficult to get additional training in suicide assessment and management after graduation. Individuals who feel they need additional training are forced to pick and choose from an array of conflicting sources of information, various schools of thought and a narrow range of research findings. From these sources they must glean what they can and try to apply it clinically. This virtually ensures that there will be tremendous diversity among practicing clinicians concerning even the most basic aspects of suicide assessment.

As managed care and other cost-containment efforts become the driving force behind the provision of many social services, professionals without doctorates (for example, nurses, drug and alcohol counselors, therapists, student advisors and correctional workers) will have to play an even larger role in the delivery of services, shouldering clinical responsibilities for which they are minimally prepared. For these practitioners, formal training is even less available than it is for those with doctorates.

Because they are often the first to come into contact with potentially suicidal individuals, they will have to make assessment decisions with little or no practical knowledge. This is not only unfair to them, it can be fatal to their clients.

LEGAL HAZARDS

Perhaps one of the most serious hazards of working with potentially suicidal clients is the threat of litigation. Malpractice lawsuits against mental health professionals have skyrocketed over the last 20 years — and the failure to prevent suicide is the most common cause of litigation against all mental health disciplines, including doctors, nurses, psychologists and social workers. As a result, clinicians must not only deal with the extraordinary emotional pain that can arise when one of their clients kills himself, but now they must also worry about the very real possibility of being sued. And this is not an exaggerated concern. In a five-year analysis of lawsuits brought against psychiatrists, there were more claims resulting from the suicide of a patient than from any other cause, and these lawsuits resulted in the largest financial settlements (Robertson, 1988).

Furthermore, any mental health care provider can be sued at any time, for any case, regardless of the actual merits of the case and regardless of the quality of his performance during the assessment. In the courtroom, the plaintiff's attorney is free to challenge every aspect of the assessment to prove his claim. Not only will a clinician's determination of a client's suicide risk be investigated, but so will the processes and methods he used to reach it. In fact, the methods he used to reach his conclusions about risk are probably more important. Because the court realizes that practitioners cannot actually predict who will or will not commit suicide, the central legal question is not whether the practitioner was right or wrong but whether he arrived at his determination logically, using accepted professional practices.

In light of the increasing likelihood of litigation against mental health care workers in cases of completed suicide, it is surprising that so many practitioners remain uninformed about even the most fundamental legal concepts that pertain to their practice. Even though the changes that have occurred in the legal system regarding mental health providers are intimidating and the cause of a great deal of stress, it would be unfair to say that practitioners are always hapless victims of the legal system. In fact, they are often their own worst enemies, actually causing many of the difficulties they encounter in the courtroom. Instead of taking a systematic approach to determining suicide risk that is based on a combination of objective data and reasoned judgment, practitioners often make the mistake of using idiosyncratic procedures that are guided primarily by their personal ideas, assumptions and theoretical orientations. This approach leaves them wide open to the courtroom skills of fast-talking attorneys and expert witnesses who can easily dispute the procedures they followed and the conclusions they reached.

To protect themselves, practitioners must become familiar with the legal principles that affect their clinical activities. They must learn how to conduct suicide assessments that are clinically sound and at the same time within the legal standards. Unfortunately, this is easier said than done. There is not a great wealth of information on the legal aspects of working with suicidal clients and much of the material that does exist is written for lawyers, is narrowly focused and lacks practical application. To analyze and apply the information clinically requires an investment of time and energy that most practicing clinicians do not have.

TOWARD A PRACTICAL SOLUTION: THE
H.E.L.P.E.R. RISK ASSESSMENT SYSTEM

While none of these problems can be solved overnight, the assessment system presented in this book is a major step in the right direction. H.E.L.P.E.R., as this system is called, is a structured method, a clinical framework, for assessing suicidality that is logical and really very simple. It shows practitioners — regardless of the professional field in which they work — how to determine their clients' potential for suicide by systematically integrating objective data with reasoned clinical judgment.

While there are many excellent books available on the subject of suicide, there are relatively few that concentrate on assessment procedures. Most of these books, offering far more extensive and detailed coverage of suicide than this book, are extremely valuable for reference purposes, but they are not particularly useful for clinical application. Some of these books take a very broad perspective, presenting many different points of view. Others cover so many aspects of suicidal behavior that finding the information about assessment is no easy task. By contrast, this book concentrates on suicide assessment alone and presents one unified point of view on how suicide assessments should be conducted. Indeed, one of the goals of H.E.L.P.E.R. is to condense the enormous amount of suicide research and to concentrate only on the material needed to perform suicide assessments.

The idea of using a "system" to assess suicide potential is something entirely new. In fact, it is a significant departure from current practice. Despite the hesitation that practitioners may have about utilizing a system to assess suicidality — most of us are not used to working within a framework or even having guidelines to follow — I believe readers will find that H.E.L.P.E.R. will enable them to conduct assessments that are more thorough, more accurate and better able to withstand legal scrutiny.

CHAPTER 2

The H.E.L.P.E.R. Risk Assessment System

This book presents a unique suicide risk assessment system called H.E.L.P.E.R. that has been specifically designed to help mental health professionals assess suicide potential in their clients. This chapter presents a brief overview of the components of the system. As we will discuss below, the H.E.L.P.E.R. system takes a multidimensional approach that addresses all of the variables and risk factors that can possibly influence suicidal behavior and thinking. While each of these areas of inquiry is important, their significance cannot be understood apart from the others. Everyone is influenced differently by the events in their lives and it is only by examining the interaction between these events that clinicians can gain a full understanding of each client's thoughts, motivations and actions. The H.E.L.P.E.R. system offers a reliable method for obtaining information about all of these factors, understanding it and applying it to the process of suicide assessment.

DEFINING SUICIDE

Before explaining how the H.E.L.P.E.R. system works, it is important that we all agree on the definition of the behavior called suicide. Most people assume that suicide simply means the act of taking one's own life. The dictionary defines suicide as the act or instance of voluntarily or intentionally taking one's own life. The problem with this definition is that it attaches the label "suicide" to any self-initiated death, regardless of why the death occurs. Consider, for example, the difficulties we encounter if we label all three of the following cases of death as suicides:

1. A man is despondent after the death of his beloved wife and, feeling he cannot go on alone, he shoots himself in the head and dies.

2. After being dumped by her boyfriend, a young woman decides to stage a "fake" suicide attempt to make him change his mind. She takes a handful of aspirins, has an unexpected severe allergic reaction to the pills and dies.

3. A delusional psychiatric patient thinks he can fly and jumps out a window to his death.

A coroner would most likely classify all three of these deaths as suicides, but this classification only takes into account the fact that these people voluntarily caused their own deaths and not the motivation behind the acts or whether the psychological process of suicide has occurred. While all three people did indeed voluntarily kill themselves, only the man in the first example wanted to die. Even though the woman in the second example voluntarily and intentionally took the pills, she was only trying to manipulate her boyfriend and had absolutely no intention of dying. In fact, it would appear that her death was an accident. The same is true of the psychiatric patient, although in his case, he probably didn't realize that he could die from his actions. The key difference between these self-initiated deaths is intent. Suicide is not an accident or a mistake. To the contrary, it results from a purposeful desire to die. If we define suicide only as a death that is self-initiated, we will be including many people who did not necessarily want to die. A better definition of suicide, and the one used in this book, is that suicide is an *intentional act that is deliberately designed to end one's own life.* This definition is much more than semantics. It is central to the assessment process because it focuses directly on one of the most critical components of any act of self-harm — whether the purpose of the act was to cause death. With this in mind, when assessing a person's probability of committing suicide, it is essential to determine whether he wants to die and, if so, why. This means the clinician must examine the motivation of the suicidal act within the context of each individual's unique life situation.

RISK FACTORS

Because the assessment system in this book is based in large part on the identification, evaluation and clinical application of suicide risk factors, it may be helpful to discuss what exactly risk factors are as well as some of the potential limitations of using them when attempting to identify suicide potential. Over the years, researchers have identified many characteristics and variables that are common to individuals who have attempted and completed suicide. Some of these are known as risk factors. They are elements that serve to increase the potential for suicide, either directly or indirectly. Some risk factors are *potentiating* (that is, they are direct triggers for the suicide act, such as a sudden devastating loss); others are *predisposing* (that is, long-range, indirect influences on the suicide act, such as a diagnosis of schizophrenia). Individually, risk factors rarely serve to increase risk for suicide attempts or completions. Indeed, in most cases, it is only when risk factors coexist and interact with other risk factors that they increase the potential for suicide. In the same way, clinicians should not consider the lack of one or more risk factors — for example, the lack of a psychiatric disorder — to be an indication of lowered risk for suicide.

There are some limitations of using risk factors to identify suicidal people. Most risk factors have been identified after the suicide event using large groups of people and even though they represent actual epidemiological data, when applied to a single person, they may have little importance or, interestingly, the *opposite* of the anticipated effect (Motto, 1999). For example, a strong support system is generally considered a deterrent to suicide, but for the person who decides to kill himself because he doesn't want to be a burden to his family, the strength and quality of the support they offer him may act as a risk factor instead of a protective factor. In the same way, even though divorce is considered a risk factor for most people, for the person whose life improves *because* he gets a divorce, risk for suicide may actually be reduced (Motto, 1999). Because of these limitations and exceptions, clinicians must consider the unique qualities and life circumstances of each individual client in order to determine how the existing risk factors may operate, interact and affect the potential for suicide

WHAT IS H.E.L.P.E.R.?

Based on the logical integration of objective data with informed clinical judgment, H.E.L.P.E.R. is a structured system for conducting suicide assessments from beginning to end — in other words, it is a complete, easy-to-use suicide assessment "package." It is designed to help all practitioners who work with suicidal clients make professionally and legally sound suicide assessments that are based on the generally accepted risk factors and variables associated with suicide. It shows practitioners what factors they need to look for to determine risk, how to obtain this information, why these factors are important, how to apply them to individual clients, how to evaluate their relative importance and how to formally document the assessment of risk in a report. Finally, the system instructs readers about the importance of risk management, teaching them how to conduct assessments in such a way that they comply with legal standards.

A Multidimensional Approach

As mentioned above, the H.E.L.P.E.R. system takes a multidimensional approach to suicide assessment. In recent years, most mental health disciplines have moved away from the single-theory view of behavior that attributes a person's actions to one primary cause such as unconscious motivation, environmental learning or biochemical disturbances. Instead, this system takes a more comprehensive, holistic approach that sees behavior as the result of a combination of psychological, environmental and physiological factors. Referred to as the biopsychosocial model, this paradigm asserts that behavior cannot be fully understood without examining all of the many variables that shape each individual's life and character as well as examining the way in which these elements interact with each other. This model also assumes that behavior is dynamic and subject to change at any time, depending on changes in the interacting variables. Because the H.E.L.P.E.R. system incorporates each aspect of the biopsychosocial triad, it aids the clinician in developing both a comprehensive and integrated understanding of the client.

WHO IS H.E.L.P.E.R. FOR?

Even though H.E.L.P.E.R has been designed specifically for mental health professionals, it actually has broad application for use by many different people in many different professions. The system will be most applicable to mental health professionals who have formal assessment or screening responsibilities, including psychologists, psychiatrists, psychiatric nurses, family and marital therapists, counselors and social workers, researchers and all other professionals involved in identifying suicidal people. It is equally valuable to educators, students and trainees in the mental health professions.

H.E.L.P.E.R is also for professionals who may not actually conduct suicide assessments, but who need a practical resource that will show them what to look for and what questions to ask to determine whether an individual needs referral for assessment and treatment. This group includes: primary care physicians; nurses and doctors in hospitals, emergency rooms, clinics and nursing homes; emergency medical technicians; police officers; sheriff's deputies, booking officers, correctional officers and counselors who work in jails and prisons; teachers and school administrators at all levels in all settings; and human resource personnel in business and industry who are involved in developing, implementing or supervising suicide intervention and prevention efforts.

H.E.L.P.E.R. will be of enormous help to people who work in the following settings:

> private and community mental health clinics
> psychiatric wards in general hospitals
> emergency rooms in general hospitals
> psychiatric hospitals
> private practices
> correctional facilities (jails, prisons, detention centers)
> suicide prevention organizations and hotline centers
> schools and colleges
> nursing homes and rehabilitation centers

human service departments of businesses and organizations
drug and alcohol rehabilitation programs (inpatient and
outpatient)

WHY DOES H.E.L.P.E.R. WORK?

Because assessments that follow the H.E.L.P.E.R. model are
driven primarily by objective data about the client that are
based on well-researched risk factors, clinicians will feel confident that they have based their determination of risk on fact
as well as on information that is generally accepted by most
professionals instead of on their personal opinions, assumptions and theories. This not only brings consistency to the
process of suicide assessment, but assessments based on a
combination of objective fact and reasoned decision-making
are much more apt to be accurate, not to mention more difficult to dispute, than assessments based on personal opinion
or theory alone. If you are sued, this will be to your great
advantage. Furthermore, because suicide is a multifaceted
behavior that can be caused or influenced by such a wide
variety of factors, if you fail to investigate certain areas of a
client's life, chances are good that your conclusions about his
risk will not be accurate. The structured, step-by-step format
of H.E.L.P.E.R. assures that clinicians will address all of the
information necessary for a thorough assessment. Moreover,
clinicians will be able to more accurately determine and/or
recommend treatment and management options because
they will flow logically from the results of the H.E.L.P.E.R.
assessment.

THE COMPONENTS OF H.E.L.P.E.R.

H.E.L.P.E.R. is an acronym that stands for the six subjects or
steps that should be part of every suicide assessment:

H = Historical Factors
E = Environmental Factors
L = Lethality of the Suicidal Thinking and Behavior
P = Psychological Factors
E = Evaluation of Suicide Risk Potential
R = Reporting Your Findings

The H.E.L.P.E.R. system is divided into three phases:

Phase 1 = Collection of Data
Phase 2 = Analysis of Data
Phase 3 = Documentation of Data

Phase 1: Collection of Data

In Phase 1, you are directed to collect data about your client so that you can determine if, and to what extent, he possesses risk factors that are associated with suicidal behavior. Data collection is conducted in the first four steps of the H.E.L.P.E.R. assessment system — "H," "E," "L" and "P."

Step 1: "H" = Historical Factors

1. Personal History
2. Family History

Step 2: "E" = Environmental Factors

1. Demographic Factors
2. Stressors
3. Social Support Systems

Step 3: "L" = Lethality of Suicidal Thinking and Behavior

1. Intent to Die

    2. Suicide Plan
    3. Access to Methods/Means
    4. Knowledge of Methods/Means

Step 4: "P" = Psychological Factors

    1. Psychiatric Disorders
    2. Suicidal Ideation
    3. Cognitive Style

Phase 2: Analysis of Data

Phase 2 is composed of one step that is represented by the second "E" in H.E.L.P.E.R., in which you will evaluate the client's actual potential for suicide based on the information you gathered in Phase 1. In most cases, suicide is a gradual process that consists of behaviors that progress along a continuum from nonlethal to deadly. By determining where the client's self-destructive behavior and/or thinking lies on a continuum of risk, clinicians will be able to decide whether he is in danger of attempting suicide and if intervention and/or treatment is needed.

Phase 3: Documentation of Data

In Phase 3, also composed of only one step and represented by the letter "R" in H.E.L.P.E.R., you will *report* your findings and present your estimate of the client's potential for suicide as well as your rationale for making this determination. You will be shown step-by-step how to write this report, why it is so important, what information to cover, how to present the material, what to avoid and the consequences of poorly written and altered reports. This section demonstrates how a report can be written in a way that anticipates common legal problems and limits the clinician's exposure to future legal liability. Reports that follow this system will be clinically sound and legally protective.

WHAT H.E.L.P.E.R. IS NOT

As with any system, there may be a tendency to want to take shortcuts or to overextend the concepts beyond their intended purpose. It must be stressed that H.E.L.P.E.R. is not a cookbook for suicide assessment and should not be used in that manner. As discussed earlier in this chapter, risk factors cannot simply be added together to determine suicide potential in an individual. For this reason, I have not used scores, weighted factors or tabulations that provide the clinician with numerical ranges to indicate levels of suicidality. While each component of the H.E.L.P.E.R. assessment system is important to the determination of suicide risk potential, they cannot be used by themselves. Instead, you must determine how each component relates to and affects the others and then use them in conjunction with each other.

H.E.L.P.E.R. is not a substitute for a clinical examination of the data. It is a guide to ensure that all of the relevant data needed for a thorough suicide assessment are obtained, that this information is evaluated in a logical way and finally reported in a clinically and legally useful manner. In this sense, H.E.L.P.E.R. is a road map that shows the direction to take — it is not a substitute for the actual trip. To extend the analogy, I cannot guarantee that by using the map, you won't get lost. Moreover, there is no guarantee that just because you used H.E.L.P.E.R., you will win a lawsuit if one is brought against you. However, for those who use H.E.L.P.E.R. correctly, I believe the chances of conducting suicide assessments that will ultimately help those in need are greatly increased and the chances of losing a lawsuit are greatly reduced, just as using a map correctly greatly reduces the chance of becoming lost. Certainly, using H.E.L.P.E.R. is better than beginning a journey with no map and simply heading in the general direction you want to travel.

H.E.L.P.E.R. is also not a substitute for continuing education and peer consultation, nor can it compensate for lack of training. Instead, H.E.L.P.E.R. should be viewed as a clinical tool. It is a guide that makes sure that you address all of the important risk factors during the assessment process and that your clinical decisions are shaped by an objective evaluation of the data.

CLINICAL JUDGMENT

Suicide assessment involves not only the collection of relevant data, but also the integration and interpretation of that information. Clearly, this calls for careful and considered clinical judgment — it is at the heart of every assessment process, and it is certainly not my intention to challenge this idea. Indeed, it is precisely the clinician's judgment, knowledge and experience that provide the mortar that binds the individual bricks of data into a meaningful structure. However, it can be extremely difficult to explain to other parties — for example, to surviving family members or a judge — that you determined the client's level of risk for suicide by using your "clinical judgment," especially if your conclusions are based on incomplete or inaccurate information. Practitioners sometimes portray clinical judgment as a mystical, almost inscrutable process that defies logical explanation. This attitude implies that you expect other people to judge the quality of your conclusions based only on faith in your status as a professional rather than on the actual facts of the matter at hand. In my opinion, this attitude is not realistic, nor do I think it should be accepted by anyone, particularly considering the questionable reliability of clinical prediction (Stelmachers and Sherman, 1989). In light of the increase in suicide litigation against mental health professionals and the fact that suicide assessments are so frequently torn apart in court, the clinical decisions that are made during the suicide assessment process must be explainable and based on more than oblique opinions. It is true that when conducting a suicide assessment, you have to pay close attention to subtle behaviors that are not easily explained —"soft signs" such as a glance, an expression or a change in voice tone — but in my opinion, it is advisable for clinicians to try to base their clinical judgments on hard facts as much as possible. Should you ever need to defend the reasoning behind your assessment to a client's family, a court or your colleagues, you will have the facts on your side, not just your subjective opinions.

CHAPTER 3

Historical Factors

The first step of data collection — and a good way to begin each suicide assessment — is to examine the client's personal and family history, paying particular attention to the factors that have been clearly associated with suicidal behaviors, such as past suicide attempts and certain high-risk psychiatric disorders. In terms of family history, we will focus on the potential influence of the client's family environment on his current thinking about suicide. While historical factors are often one of the few objective, evidence-based pieces of information that clinicians can use to determine their clients' risk potential, they are not definitive indicators of suicide. However, when considered in conjunction with other factors that we will address in the following chapters, clinicians can use certain elements of a person's past to gain insight into his current vulnerability to suicide.

SOURCES OF INFORMATION

Before beginning our discussion of historical factors, it may be helpful to consider the sources of information that you can use to determine the client's suicide risk. Of course, you will obtain the majority of the information directly from the client, but it is never a good idea to rely on this information alone. Instead, you should also consult collateral sources such as written records from the client's previous hospitalizations and treatments and talk to the client's family and previous health

23

care providers. Not only can these sources provide you with valuable insight into the client's background and possible suicidal history, they can also offer objective facts against which you can verify his self-reports.

Sources that you may want to consult include: hospital admission records and emergency room reports, medical and therapy records, drug and alcohol treatment records, court and legal records, welfare records and community mental health service records. Information can also be obtained from persons who know the client or have recently interacted with him, such as friends and family, mental health care providers, teachers, neighbors, police officers and others who may have known or had contact with the client. These sources can provide insight into the client's current attitudes and behaviors that is often unavailable in the written record and they can offer a perspective that may be different than the client's.

During the years I worked in prisons, I frequently obtained information about my clients by interviewing correctional officers, unit staff and even other inmates. In many cases, they were able to give me very relevant information about a client's interpersonal relations and family circumstances that was not recorded in the written records. Even though they may be hard to track down or reluctant to talk to you when you do find them, it is usually a worthwhile effort. Despite the potential value of using collateral sources such as these, it is important to remember that they, too, may sometimes give inaccurate information, either deliberately or unintentionally.

In many cases, it will be necessary to obtain signed releases of information from your client before you can consult records or talk to previous health care providers and family about the client. With the growth of managed care and third-party provider networks, there are numerous issues that can arise concerning client confidentiality and the ownership of patient records. Even though these topics go way beyond the scope and focus of this section, for our purposes here, it is important to stress the need to obtain permission from the client to consult records.

By consulting collateral sources, the clinician will not only be able to develop a broader picture of the client, but will also be able to verify or refute the client's interpretation of events. Although consistency between collateral information and the client's report does not necessarily indicate factuality, this information can be used as a benchmark to judge the client's veracity. Furthermore, making an effort to incorporate all possible sources of information into your assessment of the client's risk is an indication of careful clinical care.

PERSONAL HISTORY

Because certain aspects of a person's past experiences can have important implications for his current state of mind and therefore his current potential for suicide, it is necessary for the clinician to investigate the client's personal history in detail. It is important to focus on those factors that have been clearly associated with completed suicide, such as high-risk psychiatric disorders and past self-destructive behavior, especially suicide attempts. Self-destructive behavior that does not have suicidal intent, such as self-mutilation or manipulative suicide "gestures," has also been associated with suicide risk, so it is important not to discount this behavior. A history of psychological difficulties can have profound long-term consequences for a person's self-image, his coping skills and his ability to deal with everyday life. Furthermore, recurrent or long-term patterns of psychiatric disturbance can have a cumulative effect on a person's ability to function and can sometimes lead to complete emotional exhaustion. It can also lead to erratic and failed employment, legal difficulties, poor social interactions and personal isolation. These in turn can cause loneliness, hopelessness and depression capable of producing suicidal despair. Such individuals may be prone to chronic episodes of suicidal thoughts and/or actions. With this in mind, clinicians should examine the extent to which the client's current life situation (job, health, finances, social relationships, living arrangements) has been impacted by his emotional difficulties.

History of Psychiatric Disorders

Because a personal history of psychiatric disorders — especially mood disorders, schizophrenia, substance abuse, borderline personality disorders and other personality disorders — is closely associated with completed suicide, the very fact that an individual has received a psychiatric diagnosis in the past raises his risk for suicide (see Chapter 6 for a complete discussion of psychological issues). In addition to determining whether the client has had one or more of the specific high-risk diagnoses, it is useful to determine how the disorder has emotionally influenced the client and contributed to the kind of person he is today. It is also important to determine whether the client received treatment in the past because various aspects of the client's treatment history may answer a number of questions regarding his current risk for suicide. The clinician should first seek the following basic information:

- ❑ Was a diagnosis made? If so, when?
- ❑ Did the client receive treatment?
- ❑ What was the treatment (or treatments)?
- ❑ How long did it last?
- ❑ Was the client hospitalized?
- ❑ Was it voluntary or involuntary?

It can also be helpful to determine the client's response to past treatment(s) as it may shed light on his desire to help himself and his motivation for change. It may also give you some insight into his ability to help himself. Some of the questions you might consider are:

- ❑ Did he willingly participate in his treatment?
- ❑ Did he cooperate and follow the treatment plan?
- ❑ Did he feel that treatment was necessary?
- ❑ Did he find it helpful and ultimately successful?
- ❑ How did he feel about the mental health care providers who worked with him?
- ❑ Did he see them as allies or enemies?

By asking these questions, clinicians may be able to gauge the client's degree of cooperation in helping himself as well as finding out what kind of treatment strategy would be most beneficial now.

History of Suicide Attempts

Because it is a generally accepted fact that a history of prior suicide attempts is one of the most important indicators that a person may be at greater risk of eventually completing suicide, one of the first things a clinician should do in every suicide assessment is to find out if the client has attempted suicide in the past, even if it does not appear that the client is currently suicidal. It may also be helpful to determine previous suicidal ideation and threatened or planned attempts that were never carried out.

While we often look to past suicidal behavior to assess current suicide risk, the relationship between suicide attempters and suicide completers is complicated. Even though the behaviors are obviously closely related, there are some major differences between suicide attempters and suicide completers that raise interesting questions about the degree to which prior attempts are a reliable measure of future suicide, especially when used as a single predictor. Not everyone who attempts suicide wants to die and even if they do, they may not succeed. In other words, issues such as the lethality of prior attempts and the level of intent to die also play an important role in determining the client's level of risk for completing suicide (for a full discussion of lethality, see Chapter 5). On its own, a history of suicide attempts may not be a clinically reliable predictor of imminent suicide, but when it exists in a vulnerable individual along with other high-risk characteristics, it may very well increase suicide potential.

One study indicated that approximately 70 percent of the people who have committed suicide were successful on their first attempt and the other 30 percent were successful only after they had made one or more attempts (Maris, 1981). Of that 30 percent, approximately 14 percent were successful on their second attempt (Maris, 1992). These findings present us with a frightening reality — that almost 85 percent of the people who have committed suicide did so on either the first or second attempt.

Given these statistics, it is understandable why prior suicide attempts are considered such a good predictor of future suicide. However, because the vast majority of attempters never end up completing suicide, using prior attempts as a single predictor of future suicide, without examining the circumstances and motivations for the previous attempts, can lead to an overestimation of the risk of suicide completion. As stated above, people who attempt suicide are not always trying to kill themselves and even when they are, they may inadvertently use a method that is nonfatal. In fact, as many as 90 percent of attempters do not go on to commit suicide (Clark and Fawcett, 1992). This is consistent with the finding that only 10 to 15 percent of the entire attempter group go on to complete suicide at some later date (Maris, 1981; Lester, 1989). Nevertheless, as mentioned above, when considered in conjunction with other high-risk factors, a client who has attempted suicide in the past may indeed be at increased risk for suicide.

In order to identify which previous attempters are at greatest risk for actually killing themselves, clinicians must analyze a number of factors, the most important of which are the lethality of the attempt (or attempts) and the seriousness of the intent to die. An example of a high-risk attempter is a person who ingests a potentially fatal quantity of pills while alone in the privacy of his own home, but who is rescued before he dies. These kinds of people   thwarted attempters who had every intention of dying — probably represent a large part of the 14 percent of those who are successful on their second attempt. They are probably at a greater risk for completing suicide than those who have attempted suicide with nonlethal means, such as a nonfatal dose of medication.

On the other hand, many people who make attempts are deliberately unsuccessful. Sifneos (1966) estimated that 66 percent of the suicide attempters he studied did so for purely manipulative reasons. While the relationship between lethality and intent to die is explored in detail in the chapter on lethality, for now it is important to emphasize that risk assessments should not only consider the presence of a past attempt, but also the degree to which that previous attempt represented a meaningful desire to die. An example of a person who attempts suicide for reasons other than death is a woman who, trying to make her husband feel bad for mistreating her, ingests a nonlethal dose of aspirin tablets, timing it so that he will walk in the door just as she swallows the pills. Researchers have given other reasons that people make nonlethal attempts, such as a cry for help (Farberow and Shneidman, 1961) and getting attention and recognition (Lester, 1987). The problem for the clinician, of course, is separating the lethal 15 percent of the completer population from the more benign 85 percent of the attempter population. So, while past suicide behavior does not necessarily point to future suicide completions, a history of past attempts may very well increase current risk for suicide. The clinician should ask the client whether he has attempted suicide or hurt himself in the past and he should also try to corroborate the client's statements with other sources such as friends, family and hospital records. When a client has attempted suicide in the past, the clinician should find out as much as possible about the event, including when he did it, why and how he did it, what the act meant to the client and why it failed. As we will see in later chapters, the degree of suicidal intention, the lethality risk and the overall psychological formulations of the client will help the clinician make this determination.

FAMILY HISTORY

It is generally accepted that people who come from families in which there is a history of mental illness, suicide (Brent et al., 1995; Moscicki, 1997) or substance abuse, as well as dysfunctional situations such as divorce, separation, conflict and stress, are at increased risk for suicide themselves. Increased risk for suicide attempts and completions has also been associated with family violence, physical and sexual abuse (Shafii et al., 1985; Brent and Perper, 1995).

Is Suicide Inherited?

The findings discussed above have led some researchers to conclude that suicide may be a genetically inherited trait. Unfortunately, we are nowhere close to having a definitive

answer to the question of whether suicidal behaviors are bio-
logically inherited. The few studies that address the issue either
report contradictory findings or are limited by methodological
difficulties. We do know, however, that certain psychiatric
disorders, such as manic-depression, have genetic components that may place a person at a higher risk for suicide. In
other words, no "suicide gene" has been discovered, but certain psychiatric disorders that carry a high suicide risk are
genetically transmitted. Most likely, the mechanisms by
which suicidal behaviors are increased are mediated by a
combination of psychological, environmental and genetic factors. For this reason, it is important for clinicians to ask their
clients about their family history of psychiatric disorders.

Is Suicide Learned?

Regardless of the role of genetics, there is no doubt that a
child's psychological development is greatly influenced by his
family and by the environment in which he grows up. In
other words, a good deal of behavior is learned and this is
probably true regarding the behavior of suicide. Young people observe the way their parents and other role models act
and they usually adopt their methods of dealing with situations, whether these methods are effective or not.
Theoretically, anyone can overcome any type of learned
behavior but, in reality, the behaviors, attitudes and thought
processes that are learned early in life are difficult to change
later on. These learned behaviors and ideas are often very
powerful, causing long-lasting effects on an individual's basic
view of himself and of the world. Therefore, determining the
types of learning and socialization processes that occurred
within the client's family may provide the clinician with valuable insight into the client's thinking and therefore his current potential for suicide. You can try to obtain this information by asking the client specific questions about family prac-

tices and attitudes. For example, you may ask him: How did your family deal with stressful situations? Did their methods help matters or make them worse? What did you learn from these events and how did they shape your thinking? By discovering the underlying assumptions the client uses to make judgments, the clinician may be able to better understand how the client has formed his opinions of acceptable or inappropriate behavior. It is also helpful to determine the type and degree of problem-solving skills the client learned from his family. People who come from family environments in which they have learned minimal or maladaptive coping and problem-solving skills are at a greater disadvantage when it comes to managing difficult life events. When a person is not a good problem solver and has trouble perceiving that there are various options available to him, he may come to see suicide as the only solution.

Family Views of Suicide

It can also be helpful to find out how the client's family views the idea of suicide. In some families, suicide is against religious, moral or cultural beliefs. In others, it is seen as an acceptable or at least a tolerable means of dealing with problems. This latter view may be the case, for example, with the Hemingways, in which family members from one generation to another committed suicide. Even though it is possible that depression associated with physical illness played a major role in most of the Hemingway suicides, it is also possible that the family members who killed themselves learned from other family members that suicide is a perfectly reasonable if not desirable solution to an unbearable life.

Family History of Suicide

Because a family history of suicide has been associated with both attempted and completed suicide, in cases where a family member has committed suicide, the clinician should obtain as much information as possible. Who committed suicide, when did the suicide occur, at what point in the victim's life, and under what circumstances did it happen? It is also imperative to understand the client's relationship to the deceased family member. Did the client identify with the family member, like or dislike him, see parallels between himself and the victim? The clinician should also attempt to determine the impact the relative's suicide had on the client. Did it affect him in a way that seems to increase his suicide potential or did it act as a deterrent? Did the client feel guilty or was he relieved, sad, happy or envious? Finally, the clinician must try to discern what the client learned from the relative's suicide. For example, did he learn that the family member was missed? That affection was shown after the death? That others felt guilty or sorry about or responsible for the death? It is of critical importance for the clinician to explore the full range of emotions, motivations and lessons the client may have learned and determine how those things affect his current suicide potential.

LOOKING AT THE BIG PICTURE

At the conclusion of this first step of data collection — and at the end of each of the next three steps — it can be helpful to take a step back and look at all of the information that you have gathered to see what kind of picture emerges. In the same way that you can only really get the full effect of a tapestry when you stand back from the individual strands of thread, the clinician should distance himself from the data and try to get a total picture of his client. In this sense, the assessment must not only include a careful examination of each specific piece of information, but also a look at the broader picture that emerges. Risk factors rarely act individually to increase suicide risk. Instead, it is usually the co-occurrence of many risk factors and the way in which they interact that culminates in increased or decreased risk for suicide. Therefore, it is essential for clinicians to look at all the information they have gathered and consider it as a whole. Indeed, answers to some of the most important questions within an assessment might only be gained from examining the data as a whole.

Here, at the end of the history step, the clinician might ask himself questions regarding the type of client he is dealing with. Does he have a history of high-risk behaviors and events relating to himself and his family? Has there been a history of suicide attempts and/or other dysfunction in his family history such as mental illness, abuse and divorce? If so, how does this history affect his current potential for suicide? Does his personal history increase or decrease his current potential for suicide? Has he suffered from psychiatric illness or serious physical illness or personality disorders (especially affective disorders). Has he experienced life stressors and losses that have been associated with suicide, such as interpersonal loss, legal problems or loss of a job? By answering questions such as these, the clinician will be able to gain a broader and more accurate understanding of where the client lies along the continuum of suicide risk.

CHAPTER 4

Environmental Factors

In this next step of data collection, we will examine the way in which environmental factors impact on suicide potential. For our purposes here, I use the term environmental factors to refer very broadly to the way in which people are affected by and interact with the world around them. I will focus on how demographic categories to which a person belongs (such as age, race and employment status) can increase his statistical risk for suicide and how factors in a person's current life situation (such as stress, loss and social support systems) can influence his potential for suicide. This information is based on one of the early findings of suicide research — that there are some similarities among people who have killed themselves. We know, for example, that completed suicide occurs most often in elderly, white males. We also know that many suicide completers had recently experienced a severe loss, had high levels of stress prior to their suicides and that they lacked a support system. Therefore, because it is generally agreed that suicide risk is increased as a person's demographic characteristics and current life situation more closely resemble those of completed suicides, clinicians should consider and explore environmental issues such as these in every suicide assessment.

DEMOGRAPHIC FACTORS

Even though demographic data, such as we will discuss in this chapter, are helpful, they cannot actually *predict* who might be suicidal. Despite the fact that a large percentage of people who have completed suicide had a combination of various demographic risk factors such as male gender, old age or adolescence, Caucasian race, physical illness, unemployment and unmarried status, most of those who carry these risk factors do not go on to commit suicide. Furthermore, there are many more people fitting this description who are not suicidal. If we were to use this demographic profile for purposes of assessment, we would end up identifying an artificially large number of people as suicidal when in fact most of them are not. In other words, you cannot simply conclude that if a person fits the profile, he will definitely be suicidal and conversely, that just because he does not possess these characteristics he is free of risk. Nevertheless, because people who fit this profile may indeed pose greater levels of suicide risk, it is important for clinicians to consider the extent to which clients fall into these demographic categories.

Gender

Because we know with certainty that men complete suicide more than women — at a rate three times greater — and that women make more attempts than men do, gender is an important variable to consider in suicide assessment. This gender difference may be attributed in part to the fact that men and women tend to use different methods when they attempt suicide. In most cases, because men use more lethal means than women, their likelihood of killing themselves is greater. Men tend to use firearms and hanging, while women tend to use poisons and drug overdoses. However, even when men and women use the same methods, men are still more successful in killing themselves. When women use guns, they tend to aim for the torso while men tend to aim for the head. Even though there have been various attempts to explain why men make more fatal attempts than women — such as citing sociocultural, hormonal and physiological differences — we are not certain how to account for this difference. However, the reason why gender makes a difference is not really that important in terms of assessment. What is important is that there is a clear and consistent disparity between male and female suicides that puts men at greater risk.

Age

Research shows that suicide is more common in certain age groups, especially older adults and adolescents. We know that in most industrialized countries of the world, the threat of completed suicide increases significantly with age, but the peak age is different for men than it is for women. In 1988, in the United States, men 75 years of age and older were at the highest risk for suicide, and for women, the highest risk group was those aged 45 to 65 (Lester, 1997). The other high-risk age group is adolescents. According to federal statistics, teen suicide rates have quadrupled since 1950, making the current problem nothing short of an epidemic. Below we will briefly discuss some important information for clinicians about working with clients who fall into these two groups.

Adolescents

Suicide is now the third most common cause of death among adolescents with an incidence rate of 11 per 100,000, accounting for approximately 2,000 deaths per year (Garland and Zigler, 1993). The situation is even worse if we add to this the number of young people who attempt suicide or think about it. A 1994 Gallup Poll found that 12 percent of adolescents between the ages of 13 and 19 said they had "come close" to taking their own lives, 5 percent stated that they had actually attempted to kill themselves and 59 percent reported that they knew a peer who had attempted suicide. More recent research suggests that the problem has only gotten worse in the last few years. In 1997, an estimated 9 percent of adolescents attempted to harm themselves and even more thought about it (Goldman and Beardslee, 1999). Like adults, adolescent males commit suicide more often than adolescent females, but adolescent females make more suicide attempts. The suicide rate of young people is higher among whites, but in the last few decades, the rate among young black males has increased significantly. Even though we are not certain how to account for the increase in adolescent suicide, it has been speculated that it may be due to a combination of increased alcohol abuse and depression, the increased availability of firearms and a breakdown of the family unit by divorce and separation.

For many young people, adolescence is a difficult time of life that is full of emotional turmoil, gloomy introspection, drama, moodiness and heightened sensitivity. Because these are expected aspects of the adolescent experience, it is easy for practitioners to mistake serious suicidal thoughts for normal teenage angst. There is also a tendency for parents to downplay self-destructive behavior in young people and to treat it as attention-seeking and histrionic. This is a dangerous mistake. Self-destructive behavior in adolescents may very well indicate a true desire to die and one should not assume it is anything but serious until otherwise determined. Many of the major risk factors for suicidal behavior in adults are similar to the major risk factors for adolescents, but there are some differences in young people (Garland and Zigler, 1993), the most important of which we will discuss below. One thing to keep in mind when assessing adolescents is that they are often much more impulsive than adults and may tend to make decisions that they have not carefully thought through. The danger this represents in terms of suicide is obvious. Even though adolescents, like other age groups, often give clear warning signs that they might be contemplating suicide, their tendency to act impulsively may give us less time to intervene.

Clinicians should pay special attention to their adolescent clients and should try to see issues from their point of view because it is often very different from an adult's perspective. It is of critical importance to be able to recognize and respond to both obvious and veiled clues to suicide, whether behavioral, emotional or verbal.

Depression in Adolescents

Depression is as much of a high-risk factor for suicide in adolescents as it is for adults (Spirito et al., 1989). In fact, depression may be more of a risk factor for adolescents because they tend to be more impulsive than adults and therefore, a depression may not only trigger thoughts of suicide more easily but they may act on the impulse more readily. Recent studies have shown that more than 20 percent of adolescents in the general population have emotional problems and one-third of adolescents attending psychiatric clinics suffer from depression (Fleming et al., 1993). For many young people, depression is so devastating that they can see no way to stop their pain or to extricate themselves from what seems to be a hopeless existence, except for suicide.

For a clinical diagnosis of depression to be made in adolescents, the depression must last at least two weeks and must include at least five of the following symptoms:

❏ Sleep disturbance (sleeping too much or insomnia)
❏ Inability to concentrate
❏ Feelings of hopelessness
❏ Change in eating habits (overeating or lack of appetite)

□ Hyperactivity or loss of energy
□ Serious risk-taking
□ Change in school performance
□ Thoughts of suicide and other morbid
   preoccupations

Because adolescents often display depression differently than
adults, clinicians who are not used to working with them may
have a hard time determining whether they are seriously
depressed, and therefore more apt to attempt suicide, or if
they are just experiencing "normal" teenage angst. While
many of the symptoms of depression in adolescents are the
same as for adults, adolescents may present their symptoms
differently. For example, adolescents may show depression
through conduct or behavior disorder, missed classes and/or
a drop in grades, anorexia or bulimia, boredom, preoccupation with music and musicians with nihilistic themes and
other forms of creative expression with morbid themes.
Adolescents may also display other symptoms when they are
depressed, such as promiscuity or lack of sexual interest, and
they may also experience physical symptoms, especially
stomachaches and headaches. When assessing adolescent
clients, the clinician has the difficult task of deciding which
of them will be able to deal with depression constructively —
or at least pull through relatively unscathed — and which
ones might try to kill themselves over it.

Family History of Adolescents

It is of utmost importance for the clinician to look into the
adolescent's family history. If an adolescent has a parent (or
parents) with a psychiatric disturbance or a history of depression, substance abuse and suicide attempts, then that adolescent
may be at an increased risk for suicide himself (see Chapter
3, Historical Factors, for a further discussion of this subject).

Also, if a member of a young person's family has committed suicide, it can be extremely helpful to examine the way in which the client responded and the way in which it may have affected his current thinking about the act of suicide. Perhaps family suicides have caused him to see suicide as an acceptable means of coping with problems and therefore he may be more apt to choose this method himself. If parents have psychiatric or substance abuse problems, it may mean that the child is trapped in a chaotic and difficult environment, making him subject to unusual stress. Family troubles may also cause youngsters to feel unloved and unwanted and may make them doubt their self-worth. Other factors that have been associated with an increase in suicide rates among adolescents are the loss of a parent from death, separation or divorce, the emotional withdrawal of the parent, poor parenting, and sexual and physical abuse.

Risk Factors and Triggers for Adolescent Suicide

There are other important differences between adolescents and adults that clinicians need to take into consideration. For example, whereas suicide among adults is often related to illness and chronic, long-term personal issues, in young people it is more often related to acute interpersonal problems. The breakup of a romance to a teenager can be so completely devastating that it can trigger suicide. This kind of problem may seem relatively insignificant to most adults, but to adolescents, it can seem so terrible that life is not worth living anymore.

When we don't know why a person committed suicide, the only way we can research the psychological processes that led up to the act is by conducting a *psychological autopsy*. In this method of research, the family, friends and doctors of the deceased are interviewed and an attempt is made to figure out what happened in the days or weeks immediately preceding the suicide. From psychological autopsies that have been conducted on adolescents, we have learned that there are quite a few issues that triggered their suicides. The following is a list, in no particular order, of triggers and factors that may contribute to an increased risk of suicide in adolescents:

- ❑ Problems in school
- ❑ Physical, sexual or emotional abuse
- ❑ Use/abuse of drugs and alcohol
- ❑ Loss of a parent (from death, divorce or abandonment)
- ❑ Loneliness and feelings of alienation
- ❑ Feelings of hopelessness
- ❑ Suicide of a loved one, role model or mentor
- ❑ Recent disappointment or loss
- ❑ Strife or conflict within the family
- ❑ Lack of successful life experiences
- ❑ Lack of confidence and self-esteem
- ❑ Easy access to guns
- ❑ Legal problems
- ❑ Moving
- ❑ Loss or disruption of normal social networks
- ❑ Lack of role models
- ❑ Physical illness, especially AIDS
- ❑ Homosexuality

When conducting suicide assessment interviews with adolescent clients, clinicians must investigate the existence of any of these risk factors and triggers by talking to the client as well as consulting collateral sources such as parents, teachers and siblings.

Older Adults

Even though people who are 65 and older commit suicide

more than any other age group, the problem is not accorded nearly as much attention as it deserves. Each year in the United States, over 6,000 people aged 65 and older take their lives (Lester and Tallmer, 1994), and when you take into consideration the high rate of underreporting and misreporting of suicide for this age group, the number of suicide deaths is probably much higher. Also, because elderly people tend to be more serious in their intent to die, they use more lethal means and are more successful in completing their attempts than younger people (Miller, 1979).

Statistics show that for white males — the group that commits most of these suicides — the suicide rate increases with age, the highest rates being in the age range of 75 to 85. For black men, however, the peak is young adulthood, after which it drops off and then peaks again in later life. For women, the suicide rate peaks at a much earlier age, approximately 45 to 54, and drops off thereafter.

Talking with Older Adults

One thing to keep in mind when dealing with elderly clients is that they are often suspicious of the entire idea of therapy and they may be reluctant to talk to you and to express their feelings. Therefore, you should make an effort to be patient and to give them enough time to say what's on their mind. However, even when an older person does open up to the clinician, he may not come right out and say what is on his mind. For example, if he's depressed, he may say he has trouble sleeping or complain about physical ailments. Therefore, with elderly clients, it helps to try to read between the lines in the same way you would do with adolescents who may display depression in indirect ways.

Risk Factors for Older Adults

While most of the suicide risk factors that exist for other ages apply to older adults, there are a number of risk factors that have special relevance to older adults.

Physical Illness

The presence of serious physical illness plays a major role in the suicides of elderly people, especially for older men, and it is therefore important for clinicians to determine the status of the elderly client's physical health. Studies have shown that the following problems were more often associated with suicide among the elderly: disorders of the central nervous system (such as Huntington's disease, multiple sclerosis and epilepsy); cancer, heart and lung disease; hepatic cirrhosis; rheumatoid arthritis; and in males, urogenital tract disease (e.g., Lester and Tallmer, 1994).

Perhaps even more important than simply determining status of health, the clinician should find out how older clients perceive their condition or prognosis. Obviously, if they are indifferent to a fatal prognosis, the illness is not an issue of importance. On the other hand, if an elderly client is very frightened of the pain that he fears will only get worse or if he has been battling a terminal illness for a long time and is simply worn out, then this may be an important risk factor that the clinician should take into consideration.

Substance and Alcohol Abuse

Substance abuse by the elderly is often abuse of drugs they have been prescribed by their doctors. It is not uncommon for elderly people to see many different doctors, each of whom gives them a prescription for medication. The result is that elderly people have medicine cabinets full of drugs, which, when taken together or in large quantities, can be lethal. Sometimes they may not remember what they've taken and sometimes they deliberately take too much to dull the pain. The other substance that is most abused by elderly people is alcohol. Alone it can be terribly destructive; together with pills it can be lethal. When assessing elderly clients who are clearly distressed, you should make an effort to determine which medications they are taking and whether they are taking them in the right quantities. You may find that they themselves are often not sure, so it makes sense to contact the doctors they are seeing or may have seen in the recent past.

Current Life Situation

Clinicians should make a point of investigating the elderly client's current life situation — both in terms of how it really is and how the client perceives it. Has he had a recent loss (or losses) or suffered unusual recent stress? Does he have a serious physical illness? Does he lack social support systems? Does he live alone and feel abandoned and helpless? Has he recently lost a loved one without whom he feels he cannot go on? Stillion and associates (1989) noted that the effect of the accumulated recent losses of spouses, relatives and friends in rapid succession, without sufficient time to grieve each individual loss, is a great source of stress to the elderly. They also suffer the loss of physical and mental capabilities, and may face retirement, inadequate income, social isolation and loneliness. These stressors can cause severe loss of self-esteem.

Some people believe that suicide among elderly people is generally a rational act, a response to poor or failing health, the loss of family and friends, and general world-weariness. It is a mistake for a clinician to think that depression is an expected part of old age and not accord it the importance it deserves as a high-risk factor for suicide.

Race

Caucasians complete suicide more than any other racial group. In fact, white Americans commit suicide twice as often as black Americans. Even though Caucasians have the highest suicide rates, there are other groups that have displayed alarming increases in suicide. Recently, for example, there has been an enormous increase in suicide rates of African Americans, especially young men. Federal statistics show that between 1980 and 1990, the suicide rates for black men between the ages of 15 and 24 increased 63 percent, compared to the less than 10 percent increase for other racial groups of the same ages and of both genders. Even more disturbing is the fact that between 1980 and 1993 there was a 358 percent increase in suicide rates among black males aged 10 to 14, compared to a 73 percent increase for same-age whites. The Centers for Disease Control and Prevention predicts that if this trend continues, the suicide rates among young African American males will soon exceed those of white males of the same age group. Other groups that have shown increasingly high rates of suicide include several Native American tribes, attributed in part to poor social integration and acculturation.

Marital Status

Studies have shown that married people commit suicide much less frequently than single, widowed, divorced, or otherwise unattached people (Stack, 1992). Suicide occurs more often among the widowed and most often among the divorced (Dublin, 1963). Among widowed people, the death of a spouse may act as a trigger for suicide. In fact, one study reports that there are more deaths by suicide in the first four years of widowhood than the number due to all other causes (MacMahon and Pugh, 1965). This is true for both men and women and for people of all ages, except perhaps adolescents. This suggests that people with limited or nonexistent social ties may be at a much greater risk for suicide.

Illness

Although there is some disagreement on this subject, most of the research supports the idea that people who have an illness tend to commit suicide more frequently than do people who are healthy. One research team reported that up to 70 percent of completed suicides had some form of medical condition at the time of their death (Dorpat and Ripley, 1968), including chronic pain and terminal illnesses, but suicide has also been reported in those with minor conditions. There is also some evidence that people with AIDS are at significantly greater risk for suicide. One early study reported that AIDS patients commit suicide at a rate estimated to be 16 to 36 times higher than the general population (Kitzer et al., 1988; Marzuk et al., 1988). The period of greatest risk for people with AIDS appears to be shortly after the initial diagnosis.

Unemployment

Research strongly suggests that suicide rates are higher among people who are unemployed, but the reasons for this are complicated and a direct cause and effect relationship is difficult to establish. For example, when considering the relationship between unemployment and suicide, we must consider the possibility that a person might be unemployed because he is suicidal, or he might be suicidal because he is unemployed. In the same way, people with psychiatric problems may be more likely to have a history of unemployment, but they also have a history of more suicide attempts than do those without psychiatric problems. Furthermore, dysfunctional individuals may be more likely to lose their jobs and they may also be less likely to be rehired. One study found that unemployed men who attempted suicide were more often unmarried, with a history of drug abuse and a criminal record, than were employed suicide attempters (Platt and Duffy, 1986). Nevertheless, for most people lack of employment is not a desirable situation, and it usually implies a lack of income as well as a lowered sense of self-worth. For people who see their work as more than just a job — it is their profession and it provides them with an identity — loss of a job may mean loss of identity. In conclusion, unemployment alone is not likely to be a cause of suicide, but when combined with other stressors and personal inclinations, it may contribute to an increased risk for suicide. As such, it is important for the clinician to find out about the client's employment situation, both past and present, and whether it is adversely affecting him.

LIFE EVENTS AND LIFE CIRCUMSTANCES

In this section, we will look at issues relating to the client's current life situation and the way in which he interacts with the world around him. Even though there is not a great deal of research on the association between suicide and life events and between suicide and social support, the literature suggests that these things can play an important role in the process of suicide both in terms of acting as a risk factor and a precipitating factor. By exploring the events that have been associated with suicide that are currently occurring in the client's life (e.g., illness, loss of a loved one, loss of a job, home, children, money), the clinician may be able to determine whether these things are increasing his vulnerability to or triggering the act of suicide.

Life Stressors

Social and interpersonal life circumstances that cause intense pain, anguish, guilt, shame, fear and helplessness have been strongly associated with suicide, especially as a triggering event. For this reason, clinicians should make a point of finding out if their client is currently experiencing (or has recently experienced) severe stress. The kinds of recent stress that have been found in completed suicide often involved interpersonal loss and physical illness. Also, being involved in humiliating events such as a scandal, being arrested, being fired, having legal problems and experiencing financial ruin are stressful issues that preceded suicide (Hirschfeld and Davidson, 1988). Clinicians should be direct when they question their clients about any of these known stressors, being careful to cover marital, legal, financial and occupational issues.

Before discussing the kinds of stressors that have preceded suicide, it is important for the clinician to consider the fact that the kinds of stressors people encounter are not as important to their potential for suicide as the way they react to those stressors. People suffer major stressors all the time and most of them do not respond by committing suicide. What is it that causes some people to choose suicide, while others are able to find constructive coping methods? Stress is a highly subjective feeling — the person experiencing it ultimately defines it. It may be that the difference in suicidal people's reactions to stressful events is related to how they interpret themselves and the world around them. People's attitudes toward themselves are often based on their perception of how other people feel about them. With a diminished sense of self-esteem, suicidal people may easily interpret other people's perceptions as negative and hurtful. Clinicians should also evaluate how the client feels about his ability to cope with stressful events. Compared to nonsuicidal persons, suicidal individuals typically feel more overwhelmed by their perceived stress; they are less able to cope with stress and they experience significantly more emotional discomfort because of their inability to resolve their stress. The end product of these futile attempts to cope can be feelings of hopelessness, leading to an uncontrollable sense of failure, worthlessness and despair

Researchers have found distinct differences in reported levels of life stress between suicidal and nonsuicidal individuals (e.g., Ellis and Ratliff, 1986). Compared to their nonsuicidal counterparts, suicidal individuals more often report experiencing life stress and they more often believe that they have been dealt a bad hand and burdened with ill fortune. Knowing this, clinicians should seek to determine the degree to which clients perceive themselves to be under significant life stress, regardless of the objective reality of the situation.

For most people, the most significant source of stress in life is change. Change is, of course, an inevitable consequence of life. Sometimes it is planned and sometimes not. Change can affect us in either positive or negative ways. Perhaps the most predictable change is the normal developmental transitions that we all encounter in life as we age. Teenagers must eventually abandon adolescent coping strategies and learn to develop more adult ways of dealing with life. Young adults must learn to take care of themselves, to function in the working world and to become parents. Older adults must face the challenges of decreasing physical abilities, declining health and, often, having to rely on others to care for them. To cope effectively with these natural life transitions, we must be flexible in the way we confront change. New skills must be substituted for old ones and more sophisticated coping strategies must be learned to replace no longer effective or pertinent methods.

As we will discuss in Chapter 6, Psychological Factors, there is a good possibility that the personality-related disorders that are characteristic of suicidal people make it difficult for them to adapt to these necessary developmental changes, increasing their inability to cope, which in turn increases stress. Their cognitive rigidity and problem-solving deficiencies make it only harder for them to adjust to life events. Add to that an inability to escape the feelings of personal inadequacy and social separation that often accompany these problems, and the option of suicide becomes more appealing and therefore, in terms of assessment, more likely.

In some cases, what seems to be external stress is really self-generated stress. For example, some people perceive themselves in terms of how they think other people perceive them. To gain approval, they ignore their own needs and instead strive to meet the standards and expectations that are set by other people, whether these are parents, employers, peers or spouses. For example, a woman may try to meet the high expectations set for her by her boss as an employee, set by her husband as a wife and by her children as a mother. Because each set of expectations is very demanding (and in some cases contradictory), she may find herself unable to meet all of them. This may cause her to feel like a failure in any one or all of these situations, regardless of her actual level of performance. Driven to meet the expectations of others, she tries harder and harder but may only fail more and more. Living under these conditions over long periods of time can lead to physical and emotional collapse. In these situations, suicide can be seen as an escape from the intolerable, unrelenting pressure to perform.

When faced with overwhelmingly stressful situations for

which they are completely unprepared, some people discover that their coping skills are not equal to the task. For instance, people who find themselves in chronically unrewarding, unfulfilling or abusive relationships endure extremely high levels of daily stress. In cases of prolonged sexual and emotional abuse or of perpetual family and interpersonal upheaval, suicide may seem like a welcome relief from the mental anguish and pain. In many cases, after weighing the costs and benefits, people may simply decide to kill themselves rather than live under this constant emotional strain.

Loss

It is a known fact that many people who have committed suicide had recently suffered a major loss. The losses most often associated with suicide include the loss of a loved one to death or separation, the threatened loss of a lover, the loss of a job or a home, loss of freedom, and the loss of health or physical ability because of sickness or injury. There is also emotional or psychological loss, such as loss of identity, self-esteem or personal respect, all of which can be more devastating than material loss. Another loss that may be important in the development of suicidal behavior is the loss or disruption of an important relationship. It has been reported that this is especially true for women, even though changing sex roles are making this gender difference less obvious (Canetto, 1992-93). In fact, it has been recently suggested that the breakup of a relationship is much more devastating to men (Lester, 1997).

However, as some researchers have suggested (e.g., Maltsberger, 1988), the level or nature of a loss may not be the factor that determines whether a person will become suicidal; rather, it may be an individual's ability to cope with the loss. Other researchers have suggested that the determining factor may have something to do with the way people view themselves through the eyes of others.

Furthermore, it is sometimes difficult for the clinician to understand what is causing a person psychological pain. His present feelings may not necessarily be associated with a current loss and may be caused by past experiences, making it difficult for the clinician to make the connection. For some people, the anniversary of the death of a loved one or of any other significant loss may cause a renewed sense of loss and this is also true when a certain season comes around in which a traumatic past event took place. Also, because feelings and responses to loss are highly personal, the clinician may not understand what is causing his client distress. Therefore, while it is important to explore the nature of any immediate personal losses, it is also important to consider the deeply personal emotional losses the client may be experiencing from past events.

Social Relations and Social Support Systems

Research has shown that people with low levels of social support are more likely to complete suicide than those with a lot of support (Dooley et al., 1989) and that people with limited or nonexistent social ties may be at a much greater risk for suicide. In some cases, when individuals have a social network of supportive relationships, it acts as a buffer against adverse events and therefore may be considered a protective factor in terms of suicide. A strong support system gives people a sense of belonging, a feeling of being needed and therefore a reason for living. Clinicians should therefore investigate the quality of the client's social relationships and whether the client has a useful support system, both in terms of availability and quality. The clinician should also investigate the status of the client's current social relationships and perhaps the best way to do this is to ask him directly. Does he live alone? Is he married? Divorced? If he lives alone, does he have close friends or family?

It is important to look at support in terms of a resource that the client perceives as able to provide him with physical and/or emotional assistance — whether it is a place or a person. This is a necessary distinction because support must be perceived before it can be used. Support that is not perceived as available or support that will not be sought is not support at all. Therefore, the availability of support must be based on the *client's perception* of what is available, not on what others perceive as available.

Even though there is not a great wealth of research on social interaction in completed suicides, most of the studies that have been conducted show that their social relationships were deficient. This may have been caused by the inability of these individuals to create or maintain relationships with others or perhaps it was caused by other reasons such as other losses or psychiatric disorders (Heikkinen et al., 1993). As Lester (1997) points out, there are quite a few differences in the social relationships of suicidal people.

> The problems of social adjustment that are reflected in the marriages and divorces of suicidal persons are characteristic of their relations not only with their marital partners but also with people in general. People who are at high risk for suicide tend to have been unable to maintain warm, mutual relationships throughout their lives. They do not seem able to express their need to be dependent and receive help from others, in spite of the fact that their dependency needs are perhaps more urgent than those of nonsuicidal persons. The

result of this inability to express powerful needs is, of course, that the needs remain unsatisfied. The lack of gratification is intensified by the fact that even when others go out of their way to be supportive, suicidal people tend to retreat or deny that any help is being offered. Perhaps because of their inability to express dependency needs, suicidal people often feel socially isolated to a greater extent than do nonsuicidal persons. Suicidal people tend to believe that the people with whom they have close relationships feel negatively about them.

When assessing the quality of support available to the client, clinicians must also make several practical determinations. Who is providing the support? What is the nature of the support and, if it is a place, where is it located? Does the client have specific individuals such as family or friends who are willing and able to assist him on a consistent basis? Or does he have to rely on support that may be haphazard or intermittent? For those without family or peer support, do they have access to alternative sources of support such as social service agencies, self-help groups and volunteer organizations? If a client is currently residing in an institution such as a prison or hospital, the clinician should determine whether the client can and will use the support that is offered there. Also, for support to be useful, it must be consistently available. In other words, the clinician must determine if the support is time-limited, person-limited or otherwise unavailable when it is needed. Clearly, it is of little value to have a readily available support system that will only be available for a short period of time.

Another important question to answer is whether a client is able to utilize a resource even if it is available. This may mean determining whether the client knows how to make arrangements for getting support and whether he knows how to determine costs for services or the requirements for using specific services. In some cases, service availability might mean determining something as simple as whether the client can get to a specific location and whether there *are* services at that location. Of course, none of this means much if the client doesn't want to use the services that are available, so this is an important question to ask him. While making these determinations can be difficult and time-consuming, making assumptions about them can be very dangerous if you are wrong.

Take the following example of a man who was admitted to a psychiatric hospital after threatening to commit suicide. Several weeks before the admission, his wife told him that she wanted a divorce and that he had to move his belongings out of their home. He had no friends or relatives with whom he could stay, but was able to find temporary housing with a coworker. He felt very isolated and because he did not have a phone or a car, he had no one to talk to and no way to get to a place where he could obtain help. He was very distraught and lonely and began drinking heavily. One night after drinking alone for many hours, he became very upset about his impending divorce. He put his gun in his pocket and went to his wife's home where he threatened to commit suicide if she did not reconsider her plans for a divorce. After a loud and tearful argument, she eventually called the police and had him taken to a psychiatric hospital where he was admitted. The next day, the man told the attending psychiatrist that he was fine, that he was not really suicidal and that he had only been trying to scare his wife into taking him back. The psychiatrist must have thought that this made sense, because when the man requested release from the hospital, he granted it. Within five hours of his release, the man shot and killed himself.

The psychiatrist's decision to release the patient from the hospital so soon after an obvious crisis such as this suggests that he performed a very limited assessment that did not take into account the man's total life situation. In fact, it appears that the psychiatrist's decision was based exclusively on the client's verbal statement that he was not suicidal. If the psychiatrist had made even a cursory check, he would have easily learned that the man had just experienced significant psychological and material losses, that he had no source of emotional support and that he evidenced an increasing pattern of alcohol abuse. What may have been the psychiatrist's biggest mistake was that he failed to recognize the man's total lack of a meaningful support system to help him adjust to the immediate crisis he was facing. The outcome of this case shows why it is so important for a clinician not to take at face value a client's statements about his intentions and why it is so necessary to find out from additional sources what might really be going on in the client's life. Clearly, this was a very involved case that includes a number of risk predictors. However, it is not unique to an inpatient psychiatric setting. It is also quite typical of the cases in which a client suddenly arrives at a hospital emergency room or a mental health clinic for evaluation, or cases that lead to an arrest and overnight detention in a county jail.

As this case demonstrates, determining suicidal intention by relying exclusively on the statements of a distraught client can be very dangerous to the client and both professionally and legally problematic to the clinician. Prior to making the decision to release the patient, the psychiatrist, knowing as he did that the man had been intoxicated and brought to the hospital by the police, could have followed up with a call to the police to obtain more information. With sufficient questioning (and appropriate concerns for confidentiality), he would have been able to determine that the man was highly distraught by the problems he was having with his wife, that he had been thrown out of his home, that he had threatened to kill himself, that he had been drinking to excess in the weeks prior to the incident, and that he had no source of support whatsoever.

Had the psychiatrist known the severity of the man's problems and the fact that he had nowhere to go for help, he almost certainly would not have released him from the hospital. The overriding concern is whether the client has meaningful emotional and social attachments to others. Those with an available, intact social support network, particularly friends and family, are more likely to have better and more abundant resources to draw on than those with limited attachments. Therefore, it is not surprising that those with better systems of support are less likely to complete suicide.

CHAPTER 5

Lethality

A suicide assessment must look at more than just a person's risk for attempting suicide; it must also determine the probability that death will occur as the result of the attempt. This is generally referred to as lethality. Lethality is increased (i.e., there is a greater chance for death) when a person has a good plan, when he uses a deadly method and when he has the skill to carry out the act and the knowledge to determine the effectiveness of the chosen method. However, except under the most extraordinary of circumstances, by themselves, these factors will not usually cause death. Indeed, without a desire to die, most people will not try to kill themselves in the first place. Therefore, to assess the probability that death will occur as the result of a suicide attempt, clinicians must consider both the deadliness of the plan and the intensity of the intent to die. Only then will the clinician be able to obtain a complete picture of the client's overall self-destructive potential.

COMPONENTS OF LETHALITY

In most cases, if a person has developed a good *plan* and he has the *means* and *knowledge* to carry it out, his chances of dying from a suicide attempt are greatly increased. But, as we will discuss below, rarely will these three components come together to cause self-inflicted death without *intent* to die. If someone is seriously intent on dying, one way or another, he will usually find a way to achieve his goal. If he doesn't get it right the first time, chances are good that he will the next. In fact, of people who have committed suicide, 84 percent succeeded in killing themselves by their second attempt (Maris, 1992).

However, while intent is a very important factor in completed suicide, it is a mistake to assume that it is the single determining factor. There are various reasons why some people die when they attempt suicide and others do not and these reasons sometimes have nothing to do with the level of a person's suicidal intent. It is always possible that an error, a misjudgment or an accident will occur that causes a determined suicide attempt to fail or an ambivalent attempt to succeed. For example, a person who truly wants to die may unintentionally choose a nonlethal method because he doesn't know any better, and a person who is engaging in self-destructive behavior for the sole purpose of frightening someone may inadvertently take too many pills. While intent and knowledge can greatly influence the outcome of a self-destructive act, the physical dangerousness of the attempt can also be an extremely influential factor and therefore must be considered by the evaluating clinician, regardless of the level of a client's intent. Clinicians cannot rely on any one factor to assess an individual's current potential for completing suicide. Rather, they must examine the combination and interaction of all of the components of lethality.

Lethality is a multifaceted concept that involves the interaction of the following components:

> **INTENT:** Having the desire to die
> **PLAN:** Having a strategy to commit a deadly act
> **MEANS:** Having access to the means needed to commit the act
> **KNOWLEDGE:** Having information and skill necessary

to use the means effectively

An easy way to conceptualize the relative importance and interaction of the components of lethality is by means of the following lethality equation:

LETHALITY = Intent to Die (Plan + Means + Knowledge)

Of course, none of these components is static, nor are their relationships predetermined; therefore, the lethality of a person's self-destructive behavior and thinking is ever-changing. Any one or all of these components can change at any moment, as can the way they interact with each other. The lack or addition of a component may serve as something that either prevents or provokes suicide. If, for example, a person's intent grows stronger, his risk is usually increased. Or, if a person suddenly loses access to the lethal method he was planning to use in his suicide attempt, his risk will usually diminish. However, one cannot make assumptions about lethality based on the value of one component. While a person's intent may increase, his plan may fall apart. For this reason, to accurately assess lethality, the clinician must address and weigh each component of the lethality equation to determine its relative strength and relationship to the others. In most cases, for a completed suicide to occur, the four components must come together in a particular way and in a particular moment in time. Therefore, determining an individual's current suicide risk potential requires an examination of the *current* relative strength of each of the elements and their *current* relationship to one another.

Intent

Intent to die — or the seriousness, intensity or degree of sincerity of one's suicidal wish — is the factor that most directly affects the likelihood that death will occur. Therefore, to emphasize its relative importance in our lethality equation, intent is represented as a multiplicative rather than an additive element. Without a desire to die, it is unlikely that a person will even try to kill himself (unless perhaps the person is psychotic). Generally, the greater and clearer the intent, the greater the risk for suicide attempts and successful outcomes. People with a high level of intent are likely to kill themselves eventually even if their suicide plan is disorganized and impractical and even if their knowledge of and access to lethal means are limited.

Given its importance in assessing suicide potential, it is unfortunate that determining a person's intent to die can be such a difficult factor to quantify. It usually requires a good deal of inference and judgment on the part of the clinician. Even when you have determined that a person wants to die and have identified his reasons for wanting to die, it is still hard to know how serious he is and how strong his desire is, even after questioning him about this directly. While questioning the client about his intent is crucial and can often shed a good deal of light on the severity of his desire to die, it is always important to consider the genuineness of self-reports. For various reasons, people often try to exaggerate or minimize their level of intent and it is often difficult to distinguish the actual facts from fiction, denial, or distorted mental states. For this reason, you should also try to gather data from other sources such as friends and family (and, depending on the client's particular situation, you may be able to question a variety of other people, such as police or fellow inmates). However, in the same way that you cannot necessarily believe everything the client tells you, you should not rely on information you get from other sources because they too may give you inaccurate or biased information. Nevertheless, you can often obtain a broader understanding of a client's level of intent after a full exploration of all available sources.

In addition to evaluating the variables in the lethality equation above — suicide plan, choice of and access to means and the level of knowledge (which we will discuss later in this chapter) — there are several objective indicators that clinicians can consider to determine severity of intent. For example, intent is usually quite high if a person has written a suicide note for a planned attempt, if he has engaged in "life-organizing" behaviors in preparation for death, such as getting important documents in order (a will, ownership documents, etc.), and if he has given away cherished possessions. These indicators can also be used to evaluate the severity of a client's past suicide attempts. If he engaged in them, it may indicate that he fully intended to die and thought he would die, which is, clearly, valuable information.

There are a number of specific questions clinicians can consider to help them assess the client's level of intent:

- Why does the client want to die (to hurt someone, to end his pain, to punish himself)?
- What are the contents of his thoughts and are they associated with known high-risk factors (e.g., depression, illness or object loss)?
- What does death mean to him (reunion with a loved one, rebirth in a new existence)?
- How long has he been thinking about suicide?
- How frequent and persistent are the thoughts?
- Is he obsessed or preoccupied with the idea of killing himself?
- Can he control his thoughts?

Clinicians can often learn a good deal about an individual's level of intent by exploring the lethality of past suicide attempts as well as the lethality of any current suicide plans. If a client has attempted suicide in the past, it is possible that his intent was high if, for example, he chose a method that was highly lethal and if he chose an isolated place where he thought he wouldn't be rescued. On the other hand, intent may be less serious if he swallowed a huge amount of potentially fatal pills, but immediately called someone to alert them about what he had done. If a person has not attempted suicide in the past but currently has a suicide plan, the clinician should ask the same kinds of questions. How much planning has he done? What is the physical dangerousness of the chosen method? Has the client tried to obtain the means needed? Does his plan include efforts to avoid rescue? The answers to these questions will give you information about the level of the client's intent, which in turn will yield information about the likelihood that a current attempt will result in death.

Even though one can learn about a client's intent by looking at the nature of past attempts and current plans, it is important to remember that the method chosen does not *necessarily* indicate the level of an individual's desire to die. The lethality of an attempt or plan may easily be influenced by a number of factors such as unintended consequences, the quality of the suicide plan, the level of knowledge and the client's access to means. Also, clinicians must look at the degree to which the client *perceives* the attempt and/or plan to be lethal (see Knowledge of Methods, below). For example, even though most people would consider a suicide plan that includes ingesting 10 aspirin tablets as an extremely benign attempt, if the attempter is sure it will kill him, it should be considered a high-risk attempt — not in terms of physical dangerousness, but in terms of lethal intent. Therefore, you should always ask the client about his perception of the lethality of the method he chose as well as his expectations of actually dying from the attempt. You may want to consider asking the client the following kinds of questions:

- ❏ Did he think he was going to die?
- ❏ Did he do more or less damage to himself than he anticipated?
- ❏ Did he consider the attempt to be highly lethal?
- ❏ Does he know why the attempt failed?
- ❏ How does he feel about having made the attempt?
- ❏ Is he sorry he did it?
- ❏ Is he angry that he is still alive?

With clients who have not attempted in the past but now have a plan, you should ask them about their expectations for their plan. Of course, the level of a person's intent to die can always change. As a person's life situation and feelings change, so too does his intent and, therefore, his level of risk. The intent behind a first act does not predict the intent of the next act, nor will it foresee the lethality of future acts. While you can obtain very useful information from past acts of self-harm, each act or threat must be judged as a separate behavior.

Motivation

In order to determine whether a person wants to kill himself, as well as how much he wants to die, you must try to find out what is motivating him to feel and act the way he does. One way to explore this critically important issue is to simply ask the client why he has harmed himself or is thinking about harming himself. When viewed in the context of historical as well as current environmental and psychological factors, his responses may provide an indication about what may be contributing to his current behavior and feelings. There are many reasons why people engage in self-destructive behavior. Clearly, not everyone who engages in acts of self-harm wants to die. You must, therefore, try to determine whether their motivation is based on a true desire to die or on something other than death, such as manipulation, a cry for help, or other psychologically motivated goals. If a person honestly wants to die, risk is obviously increased, but if he has ulterior motives, his risk for suicide is usually diminished.

Manipulation

Some people threaten suicide, not because they want to die, but because they want to manipulate others, send a message to others or effect a change in their environment. Even though a suicide threat is a rather extreme method of obtaining a desired end, people do it because they have learned that it usually works. When presented with a suicide threat, most people will do whatever is necessary to prevent the threatened act. No one wants to feel as if they caused or contributed to the death of another person. The fear experienced and the subsequent concessions made by those receiving the threats are often powerful rewards for people who threaten to kill themselves.

The case of a young woman who was in one of my college courses several years ago provides an excellent example of a manipulative act of self-injury. She had recently been married and was already having problems. Her husband had become involved with another woman and had approached her about getting a divorce. In an effort to keep her husband from leaving, she impulsively took a quantity of aspirin tablets during an argument with him. She had made several previous threats to commit suicide if he left her. The woman was immediately hospitalized for depression and placed on suicide precautions. A few days later, I received a call from her husband asking me to give him her assignments so she could study for a test while she was in the hospital. After returning to class, she informed me that her husband had promised he would not leave her. Without knowing more about this particular case, it is difficult to make any firm conclusions about this young woman's motivation for taking the aspirin tablets. But on the surface, it seems safe to speculate that the act was less designed to end her life than to control her husband's behavior. To define this act as suicidally motivated exaggerates its lethality. From a legal perspective, it may be safer for clinicians to treat all clients who self-injure as suicidal, but it is bad clinical practice because it leads to a variety of inappropriate treatment strategies that are counterproductive for dealing with the issues that led to the act.

If suicidal threats and manipulative self-destructive behavior are so effective in achieving desired goals, one may wonder why people who are motivated by these reasons would ever go on to kill themselves. The answer is that after a while, these manipulative threats lose their potency, particularly if they occur repeatedly and involve minimally lethal acts. Even though the recipients of these kinds of threats are usually upset and frightened at first and therefore take the threats seriously, eventually they begin to ignore them when they see that they are only threats. They may even become angry at the threatener after they perceive the threats or acts are only being used to manipulate them. If this occurs, the threats no longer have power over others, and the threatener may feel he must escalate the severity of the threats or acts to regain control over others and to "prove" he is serious. This can be fatal because, as we have mentioned, even though a person may not intend to kill himself, there is always the possibility that he may end up dying accidentally.

People who engage in manipulative self-injurious behavior often take overdoses of medication and may also engage in episodes of wrist and arm cutting with a razor blade or other sharp objects. They usually ingest a minimally lethal medication or, if they take something more lethal, they make sure that someone is available to rescue them. Acts of self-cutting are typically sublethal and usually require minimal medical attention.

Even when you have determined that a client is threatening suicide for manipulative reasons, you cannot simply conclude that he is at low risk because there is always the chance that he will die by accident if, for example, he inadvertently chooses a lethal method or if his plans for rescue fall through. Before making a decision about level of risk, clinicians must look at all of the risk factors in the lethality equation, and should consider manipulative attempters to be at risk until they have determined otherwise. The rationale for their decision should be clearly documented in their report.

Cries for Help

Many people who talk about suicide or make attempts are actually more interested in finding solutions to problems than committing suicide. They may say that they want to die or that they are planning to kill themselves, but their real goal is often to let others know they are hurting and they need assistance. In terms of lethality, cries for help — sometimes called suicide "gestures" — are low- to moderate-level acts that have the potential to bring about death, but in most cases do not. The fact that these individuals want to solve their problems and give others a chance to intervene and prevent their suicides usually implies that they are not committed to dying. Gestures such as cries for help are usually made by people who are suffering intensely from a crisis and even though they don't necessarily want to die, they do know that they must solve the current problem.

If their gesture results in summoning the help they need to

resolve their problem, then they have succeeded, but if the gesture should result in their death, then they will not have to suffer the emotional pain caused by the problem and this too is perceived as a successful outcome. Because of their confusion, frustration and ambivalence about wanting to die, clients who make gestures such as a cry for help are subject to unpredictable and rapid emotional change and therefore are a considerable clinical challenge.

An example of a relatively serious cry for help may be illustrated by the case of a woman who had been in a physically and emotionally abusive marriage for many years. She had no immediate family to turn to for support and only limited resources. Her situation deteriorated steadily, but she was unwilling to enlist the help of others because she feared retaliation by her husband and the escalation of an already bad situation for her and her children. Finally, in an act of frustration and desperation, she took a large, lethal quantity of sleeping pills (even though she also had access to her husband's handgun). As soon as the pills began to take effect, she called 911. An ambulance soon arrived and she was taken to a hospital where she was treated for the very serious overdose and provided with resources to deal with her marital problems.

The woman's decision to use pills rather than the available gun and her call for assistance reflect her uncertainty about dying. Although there was a manipulative component to her actions, the driving force behind her gesture was not to control her environment (i.e., change her husband's behavior) but to obtain a resolution of her dilemma. This is the critical factor that separates a cry for help from other self-injurious behaviors. People who make gestures are more motivated by the desire to call attention to and resolve a seemingly unsolvable life situation than by the desire to die or control others.

In this case, death could easily have resulted from a miscalculation of the timing of the rescue call, the potency of the pills, or an inability of emergency personnel to reach the woman in time. However, death would have been equally effective in solving her problem.

From the person's perspective, a suicide gesture can be seen as a win/win situation. The problem is solved whether the person gets help or dies. On the other hand, the ambivalence felt by people who make suicide gestures indicates that they still have some hope that their problems can be solved without death and it is this hope that prevents them from making a more lethal attempt. Although they are trying to find a reason to live, they are willing to die if a solution cannot be found. However, as with manipulative attempters, this does not mean that they are without risk or even at low risk for suicide. It is always possible that if their cries go unrecognized or unheeded, they may keep trying more and more desperate methods of communication until they die in their attempt to be understood.

Self-Mutilation

Self-mutilation, frequently mistaken as a suicidal gesture, is the direct and deliberate destruction of the body without suicidal intent. Self-mutilators often inflict serious self-injury, but their reason for engaging in the behavior is not usually to cause death. In fact, some people who self-mutilate consider the behavior to be a form of self-help. Even though this behavior rarely has suicidal intent, it can result in serious injury and accidental death and sometimes people who self-mutilate commit suicide. Of all of the completed suicides in 1994, 7 percent were caused by self-cutting and other forms of mutilation (see Table 5-1).

Self-mutilation can involve a wide range of behaviors including: burning or abrading the skin, repetitive banging of the
head, hands, arms or feet, eye-gouging, finger-biting, ingesting foreign objects (razor blades, pieces of metal and glass),
inserting objects into body orifices and into the veins or flesh.
However, the most common behavior involves self-cutting.
Especially common among psychiatric patients and adolescents (DiClemente et al., 1991), self-cutting can range from
deep to superficial and usually includes cuts on the arms,
abdomen, breasts, genitals, legs, throat or face. Some of the
reasons that people mutilate themselves, whether on an
episodic or repetitive basis, are as follows:

> To relieve terrible feelings of tension (described as
>   similar to popping a balloon)
> To obtain self-control
> To obtain a sense of identity
> To regain a sense of normalcy when emotional numbing
>   has caused feelings of estrangement from the rest of
>   the world
> To manipulate others
> To express self-hatred
> To enhance sexual feelings
> To experience euphoria
> To vent feelings of anger and frustration
> To relieve feelings of stress and tension
> To relieve feelings of alienation

Self-mutilating incidents are often dramatic and can be very
disconcerting for the treating clinician. The behavior is hard
to understand and seems senseless and frightening. As one
clinician reported: "Of all disturbing patient behaviors, self-
mutilation is the most difficult to understand and to treat....
The typical clinician, myself included, treating a patient who
self-mutilates is often left feeling a combination of helpless,

horrified, guilty, furious, betrayed, disgusted and sad"
(Frances, 1987). Even though it can be very disconcerting to
have a client who has mutilated himself, it is important not to
overreact to the drama of a cutting incident or to attribute
more risk to his behavior than is called for. However, of
course, it is necessary to determine the client's reason for
hurting himself before deciding that he is not at risk for suicide. The clinician should also evaluate the act objectively
based on its *realistic* potential to cause death. While efforts
must be made to ensure the safety of self-mutilators, the clinical picture that emerges for these individuals is entirely different from those who are seeking death and their treatment
and management should reflect these differences.

Ambivalence and Cognitive Dissonance

Determining a client's level of ambivalence about living and
dying is another useful way to measure intent to die. Most
people who are suicidal experience some sort of ambivalence
regarding the desire to live and the desire to die. Ambivalence
in this sense does not mean uncertainty or indifference. In
fact, it means two contradictory attitudes that are often
equally strong. While choosing between life and death is easy
for most people, for some the mental conflict between the
desire to live and the desire to die is extremely difficult and
causes severe distress. When a person reaches a point where
his mental conflict is causing intense psychological discomfort, he is experiencing what is known as cognitive dissonance (Festinger, 1957). To resolve the agonizing discomfort
of indecision, most people must choose one course of action.
Once the decision has been made, the dissonance is greatly
reduced.

The way cognitive dissonance works can be shown by the following example. Suppose a person knows that his neighbor
has been cheating on his income taxes for years. Because he

has seen his neighbor do this year after year with no adverse consequences, he may begin to feel that he is "entitled" to the same benefits. However, suppose also that income tax fraud is against this person's basic moral values or that he fears being caught. The discomfort created by his internal conflict may eventually cause him to resolve his dissonance by choosing not to engage in tax fraud. On the other hand, if he can convince himself that the tax system is unfair and that everyone else cheats, he may feel justified in taking a small, but illegal deduction. This decision will also reduce the dissonance he feels. Furthermore, once this person has decided to cheat on his taxes, it will be much easier for him to cheat again the following year because he will be able to use the same arguments he used the last time. This time, he may even take a little larger deduction. As time goes on, it will become easier and easier for him to justify his behavior and therefore easier to cheat on his taxes.

Deciding whether or not to take one's own life is obviously a much more complicated decision and creates a much greater level of psychological discomfort. To reduce the dissonance, a decision must be made. While most people choose to live, a few choose to die. Once the decision to die has been made, the hardest part of the suicide process is over. In fact, the relative calm reported in many individuals right before they take their own lives may be attributed to the fact that they have resolved their dissonance. Individuals with a strong intent to die have usually already made the decision to choose death over life. Furthermore, once a person has justified his reasons for wanting to kill himself, it is very difficult to get him to change his mind. Even if he fails in a future attempt, he may not have a hard time choosing the same option again.

Because of the role that cognitive dissonance plays in making the decision to die, clinicians should try to focus on determining whether clients have a high or low level of cognitive dissonance about causing their own deaths. Clients who exhibit a low level of dissonance have probably already made a decision — either to live or to die. The risk that they will commit suicide may be far greater than for those with higher levels of dissonance who are still struggling with the decision.

Reasons for Living

Another good way to determine the severity of a client's desire to die is to consider the extent to which that desire outweighs his desire to live. Linehan (1983) used a "Reasons for Living" questionnaire to identify the reasons why people decided *not* to kill themselves. These reasons include:

> Belief that they could cope with and survive the crisis
> Not wanting to cause grief or hardship to their family
> Concerns about children, especially not wanting to expose children to suicide
> Fear of suicide including both the pain of dying and consequences of life after death
> Fear of social disapproval
> Moral, religious and ethical reservations

Linehan found that the respondents to her questionnaire who were more concerned with the reasons listed above were less likely to engage in suicidal behavior. Therefore, when assessing level of risk associated with intent, it can be helpful to weigh mitigating or preventive factors against instigating factors.

Unintentional Self-Inflicted Death

As we have seen, people engage in a wide range of self-injurious behaviors for a number of reasons other than a desire to die. Although a nonsuicidal motive for an act of self-harm greatly reduces a person's risk of dying, these self-injurious behaviors may sometimes result in unintentional death. When unintentional death occurs, it raises some very serious questions about the evaluating clinician's professional responsibilities and liabilities. Namely, should unintentional self-inflicted death be considered suicide? According to our definition of suicide as an act intentionally designed to end one's life, it should not. The act of unintentional self-inflicted death might be interpreted as an accident, a mistake, or merely a miscalculation, but it should not be considered suicide because it lacks the requisite intent. People engage in life-threatening behavior for many reasons, but if their intent was to accomplish any objective other than death, it is not suicide. Some practitioners (and many more lawyers) take the position that if an individual dies after engaging in intentional self-injurious behavior, then the death should be classified as suicide. While I understand this argument, in my opinion, it is only when an act is intended to cause death that it should be considered suicide. Nevertheless, even when self-injuring clients are not trying to kill themselves, clinicians should be very careful to protect them from future injury and help them find appropriate resources. Clinicians who have accurately determined that a suicidal threat or act does not have lethal intent, and who have provided appropriate intervention for that level of risk, should not be held liable if a subsequent act *accidentally* proves fatal.

The Suicide Plan

Aside from having the desire or intent to die, having a suicide plan is often the most important element in the lethality equation in that it can significantly increase the chance of death from a suicide attempt. Having a well-organized, highly effective plan may also indicate that a person has more intent to die. Although people can successfully complete suicide on impulse and without any forethought, in general, it is safe to say that without a suicide plan, a person cannot put his intent to use. In fact, the existence of a suicide plan, especially an effective one, is almost as important an indicator of high risk as are prior suicide attempts. In general, the more specific and detailed the plan, the more serious the risk.

It is important for the clinician to question the client very closely about the nature of his plan and then evaluate the likelihood of its success. While the existence of a suicide plan should alert you to heightened risk — the person has moved beyond ideation and transformed his suicidal thoughts into a concrete design — in order to make an accurate assessment of lethality, the clinician must also address other issues:

- How far has the client developed his plan?
- When is the proposed plan going to occur?
- How specific is the plan (does he have a place, time and method)?
- Is the plan effective and feasible?
- Is the client's chosen method lethal?
- Will he have access to the chosen means when he needs it?
- Does he know how to use the means?
- Has he rehearsed his plan?
- Has he taken precautions to avoid rescue?

When you have a client who has attempted suicide in the past, you may be able to obtain valuable information about his current lethality by questioning him about his previous attempts. While you cannot rely on past behavior to predict future behavior, by looking at a past plan (or plans) and determining why it failed, you may be able to learn a lot about a client's current suicide risk. You should question the client directly about the nature of past attempts and, if feasible, consult other sources as well.

Discovery Avoidance

When evaluating the potential lethality of a client's suicide plan, clinicians should inquire about the extent to which he has contemplated ways to avoid being discovered or rescued. For clients who have attempted in the past, did they try to thwart rescue? One study showed that people whose plan included precautions against being discovered were more likely to have a high level of suicidal intent than those who took no precautions against discovery (Beck, Steer and Trexler, 1989). A person whose plan involves a purposeful attempt to conceal his activities and who takes steps to significantly reduce his chances of being inadvertently discovered and rescued usually represents a higher risk for suicide. An example would be a person who obtains a large quantity of medication, checks into a secluded motel under an assumed name, tells the desk clerk that he does not want to be disturbed until the next day, disconnects his phone and locks the deadbolt on the door.

Methods and Means

Choice of Method

If a client is planning (or even just considering) a suicide attempt, his choice of method may give you important information about the level of his intent to die as well as his chances of dying from the attempt. The first thing the evaluating clinician needs to determine is which method the client has chosen and whether that method presents a high risk for danger. Table 5-1 below shows the statistics on the methods that have been used in completed suicides in the United States for all ages and both genders combined. As you can see, firearms and explosives are by far the most preferred means — perhaps *because* they are so lethal. Because poisons, wrist-cutting and inhaling car exhaust are less likely to result in death, people attempting or planning suicide by these means have a lower statistical chance of completing suicide than those who choose hanging or suffocation and a much lower chance than those who choose guns.

Table 5-1   Method of Suicide

Method	Percentage
Firearms and Explosives	60
Hanging, Strangulation, Suffocation	15
Solid and Liquid Poisons	10
Gas Poisons	06
All Other Methods (e.g., self-cutting)	07

National figures for both men and women (United States Bureau of the Census, 1994).

The next thing to determine is why a client has chosen a particular method. If a person has more than one method of suicide available to him, there is almost always a good reason why he picked one method over others. For example, if a person with easy access to a lethal means such as a firearm takes 10 aspirin tablets in a suicide attempt, it would seem to suggest that his intent was low. But before making an assumption like this, you need to determine why the lethal method was bypassed in favor of a nonlethal one. It may have nothing to do with intent. It could be that he lacked the knowledge to use the more lethal method. It could be that his plan was disorganized, that he intended to use a gun, but at the crucial moment, the gun would not fire, making him reach for the nearest means available — means that were less lethal. Perhaps he was confused and impulsively took advantage of the first method he found. Perhaps he was ill-informed and thought the aspirin would kill him. Determining why a client has chosen one method over another may reveal important information about how much he wants to die, but you cannot make assumptions about lethality based on choice of method alone. It is only part of the lethality equation and to determine ultimate lethality, you must also consider intent, plan, access to and knowledge of how to use the method. The client's choice of method can be used not only to assess the likelihood of death from a particular method, but also to provide fruitful lines of inquiry regarding the client's intent to die.

Access to Lethal Means

Whether or not a client has a suicide plan, if there is any indication whatsoever that intent is present, it is necessary to consider whether he has access to or can obtain lethal means to kill himself. The fact that approximately 60 percent of male and female suicides in the United States are committed with firearms indicates that you must always question the client about his access to firearms and especially whether he or a family member has them at home. Studies have found that risk for suicide is increased for both men and women who keep one or more guns in the home (e.g., Brent et al., 1991) and that there has been a recent increase in use of firearms for suicide among people who are under 25 years old (Price et al., 1997). It is especially important for clinicians to find out about access to lethal means when a client has a high level of intent and a plausible plan. In terms of risk management, the clinician who does not address this issue will find himself in deep water if the client should kill himself.

Clinicians should also make a point of finding out about the client's access to other potentially lethal methods such as medications. This can be done by asking the client directly as well as double-checking with recent medical records to see

whether the client has been prescribed potentially fatal medications. Especially when clients have a history of depression,
they often have easy access to large quantities of potentially
fatal drugs. Because they have been prescribed medication
for both emotional and physical symptoms, they often have
medicine cabinets full of different medications. Also, clients
who have abused drugs probably know how to get them, even
if they don't still use them. More than that, they probably
know which drugs to take and what amount has the ability to
cause death.

While you should most certainly ask clients about access to
lethal means, it is possible that they won't tell you the truth.
Especially with clients who you suspect are determined to kill
themselves and who do not want you to interfere, you should
try to confirm this information with other sources such as
family, friends and even co-workers.

Environmental Factors That Can Affect Access to Means

Certain life situations can play an important role in determining what types of means and methods are available to a
person for use in killing himself. For example, prison inmates
and hospital patients are more likely to commit suicide by
hanging because they do not usually have access to guns,
medications and poisons. In fact, in prison, hanging accounts
for almost 80 percent of all completed suicides (White and
Schimmel, 1993). On the other hand, when evaluating a client
who has immediate and constant access to firearms, such as
a police officer, a sportsman or a soldier, you should consider
him at higher risk.

Regardless of the type of environment in which a person lives,
it is important to remember that any person can successfully
acquire a lethal means for suicide if his intent to die is great

enough. Knowing this, clinicians should investigate not only the client's current ability to obtain means to commit suicide but any past attempts to access lethal means. Even if he doesn't seem to have current access to lethal means such as a gun, if he was able to get them in the past, he may be able to get them again. The bottom line is that any client who has or attempts to acquire access to a lethal means of committing suicide should be viewed as a higher risk.

Knowledge of Methods

As we discussed in the above section on intent, to evaluate a client's ability to kill himself, the clinician should first determine what the client believes is a lethal act. In other words, despite the objective lethality of a method of committing suicide, the actual severity of the act must be considered in terms of the individual's perception of what is lethal and what is not. For instance, most people would not consider 10 aspirin tablets to be a potentially lethal overdose, but to those who believe it is lethal, using this method represents a very serious act because it indicates that their intent is high. Although ignorance of the lethality of a method may save a person's life on one attempt, because his level of knowledge will most likely increase in time, his risk for suicide may also increase.

Clinicians can learn a great deal about the level of a client's knowledge of suicide methods by looking at his past attempts. It is important to determine whether the failure was caused by a lack of knowledge. For example, if a client reports that he shot himself in the leg, was it because he didn't know how to use the gun and it fired into his leg before he got a chance to aim at his head? Maybe he really knew how to use a gun, but someone interrupted him and it went off before he was ready. In other words, while you can learn important

information about a client's level of knowledge by looking at
the methods he has chosen in the past, it cannot be used as a
sole indicator of risk because of the other variables that can
come into play.

Even if the failure of a past attempt was caused by a lack of
knowledge, most people learn from their mistakes. Like any
other learned behavior, with each suicide attempt, a person
accumulates more knowledge about what works and what
does not. One researcher has shown that for people
who eventually completed suicide, the lethality of the behavior increased with each subsequent attempt (Pierce, 1981,
1984).

Of equal concern is the client who has not made any past
attempts, but who has engaged in a concerted effort to obtain
knowledge about methods and means of committing suicide.
This can include reading books and articles about methods of
suicide and discussing the matter with others, especially people who have attempted suicide themselves. Sometimes, people obtain knowledge about methods of committing suicide
without deliberately seeking it. For example, those who work
in law enforcement and medicine and those who work with
weapons, explosives and poisons accumulate a large reserve
of information about potentially lethal means of committing
suicide. When a potentially suicidal person has an extensive
knowledge of lethal methods or means, whether he acquired
this information deliberately or otherwise, he should be considered as a greater risk.

CHAPTER 6

Psychological Factors

Research has shown that suicidal individuals appear to have characteristic ways of thinking that are different from people who are not suicidal (e.g., Ellis and Ratliff, 1986; Schotte and Clum, 1987). While many of these differences are related to psychiatric illness, others are related to dysfunctional thinking styles and the ways in which suicidal people view themselves and the world around them. Although not definitive predictors of suicide in and of themselves, the psychological factors that we will discuss in this chapter are important elements that should be factored into your assessment of a client's risk for suicide.

PSYCHIATRIC DISORDERS AND SUICIDE

Because research studies have indicated that psychiatric disorders have been present in many attempted and completed suicides, it is important to include a thorough evaluation of the client's psychiatric history and his current psychiatric status in every suicide assessment. However, it must first be pointed out that there is a good deal of disagreement among researchers on the association between psychiatric illness and suicide. One study, for example, found that almost 93 percent of its subjects who had completed suicide had a history of mental illness (Henriksson et al., 1993), while another study calculated that the average percentage of subjects with recorded mental illnesses was only 38 percent (Tanney,

1992b). Lester (1992) gathered objective data on deceased subjects prior to their suicide and found that the estimates were even lower, ranging from about 5 to 22 percent. It is probably safe to say that even though suicidal people may have mental disorders more often than nonsuicidal people, it is entirely possible that some suicidal people have no mental disorder. Indeed, the absence of a psychiatric disorder should not imply lowered risk. Despite the disparity of these findings, there is general agreement on the relative risks of the high-risk disorders that have been associated with completed suicide — mood disorders, schizophrenia, substance abuse, borderline personality disorder and other personality disorders.

Although there are no objective diagnostic tests to detect mental illness, aside from observing symptoms, there are a few ways to determine if a client is currently mentally ill. You can begin by checking to see if a client has been hospitalized, and if so, there will be psychiatric records that you may be able to consult with permission from the client. You can also consult the client's family or other close associates. Aside from asking them about the client's recent history and current status regarding mental disorders, you may also want to ask them whether they have noticed significant changes in mood, behavior and appearance, as these symptoms could indicate depression or other problems associated with suicide.

Major Affective Disorders

Because major affective disorders, especially during their depressive phases, are the most common forms of mental illness found in completed suicides of all ages, it is important for clinicians to know the signs and symptoms of these disorders. A primary diagnosis of major depression has been present in as many as 70 percent of completed suicides (Robins et al., 1959; Dorpat et al., 1960; Barraclough et al., 1974), although the mean from most studies is 50 percent. There are several factors that increase suicide risk in clients with major depressive disorders. Suicide is more likely when there is more than one psychiatric diagnosis, when substance abuse and a psychiatric diagnosis coexist and when there are high levels of other psychiatric symptoms in addition to a primary diagnosis (Shafii et al., 1985; Brent et al., 1988; Rich and Runeson, 1992). In addition, there have been recent studies that suggest that anxiety and panic disorders may carry a significantly high risk of suicide, especially when they coexist with depression, substance abuse and personality disorders (Weissman, Klerman and Markowitz, 1989; Fawcett et al., 1993; Hornig and McNally, 1995). It is important to note, however, that many researchers have claimed that by themselves panic attacks are not clearly associated with suicide.

Depression

Because depression is one of the most common diagnostic correlates for suicide — with a suicide rate of more than 10 times that of the general population — practitioners should make a careful evaluation of the existence and severity of depression in their clients. One study reported that as many as four-fifths of all completed suicides had a major depression (Fawcett et al., 1990). In fact, depression is such a significant risk factor that even when it exists without suicidal ideation, it should be considered as a sufficient reason to be concerned about suicide potential.

Research has shown that there are factors that may increase risk of suicide in clinically depressed individuals. A correlation has been found between depression and the coexistence of other conditions, especially alcoholism and schizophrenia (Jones et al., 1994). Not surprisingly, the more severe and long-lasting the depression, the more acute the risk. On the other hand, it is important to realize that signs of improvement in a depressed person do not necessarily mean his risk of suicide is diminished. In fact, suicide rarely occurs during the depths of depression and is much is more likely to occur just after a depression has begun to lift. For psychiatric patients, suicide is also more likely to occur following release from the hospital when their depression is reduced. Lester (1997) suggests that perhaps people can only find the energy to act on suicide once they have emerged from the depths of depression. Roy (1982) offers that suicide may be more likely after release from the hospital because this is when people begin to re-experience the stress of the problems that caused the depression in the first place Also, when a person seems to have turned the corner on depression, it may really be that he has made the decision to kill himself and thus resolved the dissonance he felt about living versus dying. When you notice a change such as this in a depressed client, especially when it is accompanied by emotional withdrawal, constricted affect and life-organizing behavior, suicide risk may be particularly high.

Physical and Behavioral Disturbances

The way a client looks and acts can sometimes provide a good deal of information about his frame of mind, especially when his appearance and behavior represent a change from his normal style. Neglect of appearance (sudden or gradual), loss of interest in favorite activities and wanting to be alone and away from other people are very common indications of depression. Also common are fatigue, very low levels of energy and stamina, significant changes in appetite and weight loss or gain. Depressed people may simply look unhappy and be uninterested in their surroundings. They may also have difficulty thinking and concentrating, may seem preoccupied with the past, and may express feelings of extreme pessimism, overwhelming guilt or remorse, excessive self-blame, shame and hopelessness.

Emotional and Social Withdrawal

Depressed people may withdraw socially and virtually isolate themselves from everything but the most necessary interpersonal activities. Often detectable by withdrawal from once cherished pastimes and hobbies, this loss of interest can be profound. Over time, the level of withdrawal may increase and may culminate in an almost complete cessation of social activities.

Sleep Disturbances

A broad range of sleep disturbances is commonly associated with depression and while they are not, in and of themselves, indicative of depression, their existence in conjunction with other symptoms definitely warrants investigation. Some of the most common sleep disturbances associated with depression are difficulty falling asleep, frequently waking from sleep and inability to return to sleep after only a few hours of rest. While sleep disturbances are common symptoms of a number of different physical and mental disorders, because they are so often connected with depression, it is important for the clinician to explore any reported change in a client's sleeping habits.

Bipolar Disorders

It is believed that individuals with bipolar or manic-depressive illnesses are more likely to commit suicide than those in any other psychiatric group. Suicide accounts for the deaths of as many as 20 percent of those with bipolar illness and at least one quarter of people with this disorder will attempt suicide at least one time (Goodwin and Jamison, 1990). The mood swings that are typically exhibited in those diagnosed with bipolar or manic-depressive disorders can be very extreme and long-lasting and may cycle between very deep and profound states of depression and debilitating levels of elation and exuberance. Certain factors such as the severity of the depression and the type of bipolar illness may increase the risk of suicide. It is believed that for people with bipolar illness, suicidal behavior is more likely to occur at certain times: early in the course of the illness, during mixed states, during the depressive rather than the manic phase, in the recovery period and in the period following discharge.

Substance Abuse

Because research shows that substance use and abuse are consistently associated with attempted and completed suicide, it is important for the clinician to determine whether the client has a history of, or current problems with, substance abuse. Psychological autopsy studies have shown that as many as 25 percent of the people who have committed suicide suffered from alcoholism (Murphy et al., 1992), that approximately 18 percent of all alcoholics eventually commit suicide (Roy and Linnoila, 1986) and that as many as 50 percent of those who committed suicide were drinking at the time of their death (Frances et al., 1987). Also, for those without a diagnosis of alcohol dependence, there is a substantial amount of research evidence that shows that alcohol is often involved in completed suicides (Lester, 1992a).

Although we are not certain why substance abuse increases suicide risk, it is generally believed that there are several contributing factors that may have both a direct and indirect role in the suicide process. In all likelihood, risk for suicide is not increased by substance abuse itself; instead, it is probably the contributing factors related to the abuse that are responsible for increasing the risk.

Chronic Substance Abuse

Indirectly, substance abuse, especially chronic abuse, can cause other high-risk symptoms, such as comorbid depression and self-destructive behaviors, that are associated with increased risk for suicide. Over a long period, substance abuse can cause physical, psychological and economic damage that may increase suicide risk, including social isolation, loss or disruption of interpersonal relationships and support systems, loss of self-esteem, unemployment and illness.

Acute Intoxication

In addition to the long-term consequences of substance abuse, the effects of acute intoxication are believed to have an influence on the risk of suicidal behavior. In its direct role, substance use can actually cause suicide through deliberate or unintentional overdose. It can also directly influence a person's decision to commit suicide, whether by its disinhibiting or mentally clouding effects. By impairing judgment, increasing impulsiveness and aggression, and decreasing inhibition, alcohol and substance intoxication (including cocaine and LSD) can turn an ambivalent suicide attempter into a completer or can actually cause a suicide when none was intended (although these kinds of deaths are probably more accurately defined as accidents because they lack the requisite intent to die). Furthermore, because people are more likely to engage in high-risk behaviors when they are intoxicated, the likelihood of death is increased. One team of researchers found that impulsive suicide attempts were strongly related to intoxication from alcohol (Suokas and Lonnqvist, 1995). Impulsive behavior that may begin as a nonlethal, attention-seeking act, for example, can quickly turn deadly because of a person's lack of judgment and inability to think clearly or rationally while intoxicated.

Assessing the Intoxicated Client

The evaluating clinician is faced with a difficult situation if the client he is evaluating is intoxicated at the time of the interview. For example, it is entirely possible that while intoxicated and subject to the disinhibiting influences of drugs or alcohol, the client may be seriously intent on suicide, but once he sobers up, he may lose his nerve or be able to think more clearly about alternatives other than suicide. On the other hand, ironically, intoxication may actually help someone in that it can disinhibit him enough to talk to someone about suicidal intentions that he otherwise couldn't talk about. Because of possibilities like these, assessing risk in intoxicated clients can be very difficult. While you cannot take at face value any statements that a client makes while he is intoxicated, neither can you dismiss them. In most cases, however, given the unstable nature and impaired judgment of intoxicated clients, it is better to err on the side of caution. Clinicians should take precautions to protect potentially suicidal intoxicated clients until they can be reinterviewed when they are no longer intoxicated.

Substance Abuse and Depression

Psychiatric comorbidity is also highly associated with attempted and completed suicide among substance abusers, especially comorbid major depression, which has been consistently found in substance abusers who committed suicide. It has also been associated with an increase in suicidal ideation and with attempted and completed suicide (Whitters, 1985; Roy and Linnoila, 1986; Salloum et al., 1996). In fact, several studies found major depressive disorders in over 75 percent of alcoholic suicides (e.g., Murphy and Robins, 1967; Rich et al., 1986).

Assessing Risk in Substance Abusers

Because of the many variables that may increase risk in substance abusers, clinicians must make a careful assessment of these clients. It may be helpful to look at events in the client's life that may influence his current risk for suicide, including loss or disruption of interpersonal relationships and social support systems, legal or financial problems, recent illness and recent relapses in drug use/abuse. Factors relating to the client's current life style may also offer clues to his frame of mind. For example, if he is engaging in high-risk behaviors such as needle sharing, unsafe sex and other reckless behaviors, it may indicate that he feels hopeless and doesn't care about living. Also, the clinician will need to obtain a comprehensive drug and alcohol history on the client (which may require the client's permission) as well as a history of family substance abuse, if it is available or if family members will provide the information. And of course, all of the risk factors that apply to the broad range of clients also apply to substance abusers.

Schizophrenia

Although we are not certain what causes schizophrenics to commit suicide, it is generally agreed that diagnosis of schizophrenia carries a high risk for suicide. In fact, as a risk factor, schizophrenia is often considered equal to or greater than a diagnosis of a mood disorder (Tsuang et al., 1999). Characteristics common to schizophrenics who have committed suicide are past and current depression and hopelessness, a history of lethal suicide attempts, auditory and visual hallucinations, delusions of grandeur and persecution, and distorted perception of events taking place in the world around them. Schizophrenics who experience command hallucinations should be considered an extremely high risk; nearly half of all schizophrenics who have committed suicide come from this subgroup (Resnick, 1994).

Research has found several demographic, psychological and historical factors that increase the risk of suicide in schizophrenics (Roy 1982; Drake et al., 1985; Tejedor, 1987; Black and Winokur, 1988). While none of the following factors should be considered as risk factors in and of themselves, when they exist concurrently they may increase suicide risk. Furthermore, the lack of one factor should not indicate a lessened risk for suicide.

Risk Factors for Suicide in Schizophrenic Clients

> Male
> White
> Under 30
> Unemployed
> Educated
> Family history of schizophrenia
> Social isolation
> Chronic symptoms
> Prior depression and past treatment of depression
> Hopelessness
> Previous long hospitalizations (one year or more)
> Recent hospital discharge
> Prior lethal suicide attempts
> Delusions and hallucinations, especially command
>   hallucinations

Suicidal Delusions

People who have delusional thoughts about suicide and/or death are at an extremely high risk for suicide. These delusions, generally defined as fixed false beliefs, may not have anything to do with wanting to die, but instead may be the by-products of irrational thought processes. Delusional content is usually so extreme that it defies credibility, but for those who have these kinds of thoughts, no amount of logical proof or evidence to the contrary will make them see otherwise. Therefore, clients who experience delusions associated with self-harm should be considered at high risk. It is also important to determine the specific nature of the delusions as well as the extent to which suicide coincides with or supports the content or goals of the client's delusional system.

Personality Disorders and Suicide

Personality disorders, especially borderline personality disorder (BPD), but also antisocial and narcissistic personality disorders, have been associated with suicide attempts and completions. In fact, one research team believes that a diagnosis of a personality disorder ranks just below depression, schizophrenia and alcoholism as a risk factor for suicide (Soloff et al., 1994). The main features of BPD are poor anger control and impulsivity, an unusual fear of being alone, substance abuse, unstable and intense interpersonal relationships, and promiscuity. People with BPD also frequently engage in a wide range of self-injurious behavior that often causes serious physical damage, but rarely results in death (Tanney, 1992). In cases where personality disorders are related to increased rates of completed suicide, it is often because the personality disorder coexists with other high-risk disorders such as substance abuse and affective disorders. Clinicians who have a client with BPD should be careful to differentiate between those who are injuring themselves for suicidal reasons and those who are injuring themselves for other reasons.

SUICIDAL IDEATION

Aside from identifying psychiatric disorders, it is important for the clinician to assess other psychological factors that may increase a person's risk for suicide, specifically, the presence and seriousness of suicidal ideation. Suicidal ideation refers to thoughts of suicide or death which can be specific or vague, and can include active thoughts of committing suicide or the passive desire to be dead. It is believed that approximately 5 million Americans have some kind of suicidal ideation each year (Moscicki, 1989). While the presence of ideation by itself does not necessarily indicate impending suicide — or even that the person is suicidal — we know that many people who have taken their own lives did have suicidal ideation because they expressed their thoughts to others. For this reason, every suicide assessment must include a thorough evaluation of the client's thinking to determine if he is thinking about suicide, and if so, how far he has progressed on the continuum of risk.

On the other hand, if your client does not have suicidal ideation at the time you interview him, it does not necessarily mean that he is without risk. People are often evaluated for suicide potential right after they have made a suicide attempt and it is not uncommon for the client to feel temporarily relieved of his suicidal thoughts at that time. Of course, this does not mean that he will not become suicidal again. For this reason, it is important for the clinician to explore more than just the presence suicidal ideation; he must also review other factors relating to the client's potential for suicide such as lethality, psychological, historical and environmental factors.

Approaching the Subject of Suicide with the Client

One of the best ways to determine whether your client is having thoughts about suicide is to encourage him to talk to you. Most practitioners find that some of their clients are willing, if not anxious, to discuss their suicidal thoughts and feelings, while other clients find it exceedingly difficult to discuss the sensitive and deeply personal subject of suicide. Furthermore, even when clients agree to talk to you, they might not be very forthcoming and may not be honest with you. Fawcett (1988) found that of the completed suicide cases he studied, over half of the individuals denied having thoughts of suicide or admitted to the interviewer only that they had vague ideation. For this reason, it can be very helpful to also talk to family members and friends.

During the interview, if you have reason to believe that a client is thinking about suicide and he has not yet mentioned it himself, should you directly ask him if he is suicidal? In most cases, the answer to this question depends on each individual client. You should first consider each client's level of comfort and modify your approach accordingly.

Often the best approach for introducing the subject of suicide is to be direct. It is a myth that asking someone about suicide will give him the idea to try it. In fact, being open and direct with clients about suicide and showing that you are interested and do not disapprove of the behavior may make it easier for them to talk about their suicidal feelings. Also, talking openly about suicide with clients who you believe may be suicidal will show them that you are taking them seriously and that you understand that they are in real distress. This may promote the client's trust in the clinician, which in turn may encourage him to open up.

However, this straightforward approach may not be appropriate for all clients. If you feel that a direct question about suicide will cause a great deal of discomfort for the client or will cause him to clam up, you may want to try a different approach such as inviting him to talk in general terms about the sources of his distress. You may want to ask him if he is depressed. Once you get this kind of a discussion going, it may be easier to approach the subject of the client's current suicidal thoughts.

The Client's Response to the Clinician

The way in which the client responds to you as a clinician and the way he reacts to the interview in general may also provide some useful information about his underlying emotional state, his current thinking and his potential for suicide. Even though a discussion of treatment and the therapeutic alliance between clinician and patient is beyond the scope of this book, it is important to at least mention that a good therapeutic relationship is considered as one of the most important nonverbal statements indicating that a client has a desire to live because it shows that the client wants help and support (Simon, 1992).

The way the client responds may also be a good way to judge the veracity of the statements he has made to you. For example, if it seems that the client is trying hard to be a genuinely helpful participant in the interview, it may indicate that he really wants help and therefore wants to tell you the truth. On the other hand, if he seems hostile and angry about merely being in your presence, the chances are good that he will have little interest in helping you to understand his problems.

Verbal Communications about Suicide

While there are many different ways that people can express suicidal thoughts, most of them take the form of verbal communication. It is a dangerous myth that people who are seriously suicidal do not talk to others about their suicidal intent — research has clearly illustrated that they do. Robins' team (1959) has shown that 69 percent of suicide completers verbalized their suicidal intent to someone else before committing suicide and most of them made these statements within one year of the suicide. Not only did they communicate their suicidal feelings, but many of them did so more than once, the average being 3.2 times. These verbal communications ranged from direct statements of suicidal intent to very indirect references. More recent studies corroborate this early finding, but they found that an overwhelming 94 percent of suicide completers and 92 percent of suicide attempters communicated their intent prior to the act (Wrobleski and McIntosh, 1986; Wolk-Wasserman, 1986, respectively).

You cannot assume that an indirect reference to suicide is any less serious than a direct statement or that a direct statement is any more serious than an indirect one. In the same way, there is no reason to think that a client's eagerness or hesitance to discuss suicide in any way implies that he is at lower or higher risk. Everyone has a different way of expressing himself and clearly, level of intent or risk cannot be judged from the *way* in which a person communicates information about suicide. For this reason, to gauge the severity of a client's suicidal ideation, it is necessary to look at all of the pertinent variables, including his motivation, the level of his intent to die, and the presence and lethality of a suicide plan.

Indirect Statements about Suicide and Death

Sometimes people make statements about suicide or death without directly saying that they are going to kill themselves, such as: "The world would be a better place without me" and "I'd rather be dead than deal with a life like this." While these kinds of statements may represent passive, nonsuicidal thoughts that do not indicate serious suicidal intent, it is important for the clinician not to assume that this is always the case. There are a variety of reasons why people may express themselves indirectly. For example, it may be that they can *only* express their suicidal thoughts indirectly even though they are truly suicidal. Maybe they can't come right out and say they are suicidal. Maybe the verbalization makes it too real for them. Maybe the subject is just too painful or private to discuss or they're embarrassed to admit that they want to kill themselves. Maybe they don't feel comfortable talking to the clinician. On the other hand, people who make indirect and nonspecific references to suicide may very well have no interest in killing themselves and may have another agenda altogether. They may be trying to communicate the fact that they're suffering and they want help. In these cases, they may be more interested in communicating their distress than actually killing themselves or being dead. Sometimes people make references to death or dying without actually making a direct connection with taking their own life. On many occasions when I questioned clients after they made nonspecific statements about death or suicide, I soon realized that they had no intention of converting the statement into action — instead the abstract thought of being dead seemed like a quick solution to an otherwise seemingly unsolvable problem.

Whatever the reason for the indirect statement, during the course of the interview, if a client makes an indirect or nonspecific statement about death or suicide, you should consider it an indication of true suicidal intent until you determine otherwise. Because you cannot tell whether clients who make indirect statements are truly suicidal, you have to find out the thoughts and motives behind them.

Direct Statements about Suicide and Death

Even when a client tells you directly that he is suicidal — and most practitioners will probably agree that this is a disturbing thing to hear — you cannot immediately assume that he truly wants to die and that he will act on it. You must first determine why he has made this statement. While it is entirely possible that he is absolutely serious about wanting to die, there is always the possibility that he has ulterior motives such as trying to get attention or help or seeking some form of manipulative control over others. In the same way as with indirect statements, clinicians need to first find out the client's motive for making a direct statement before they can determine risk.

Assessing Content of Suicidal Ideation

To help you determine the level of risk associated with a client's suicidal ideation and verbal statements, you will need to address a variety of factors including issues relating to lethality, such as the level of his intent to die, whether he has a suicide plan, and whether he has the means and the skill to kill himself. Generally, the more frequent, the longer and the more emotionally charged the thoughts, the greater the potential risk for suicide. Therefore, you should ask the client very specific questions about the frequency, duration and intensity of his suicidal thoughts. Has the client just started thinking about suicide or has he progressed to the point that he is now determined to kill himself?

Suicidal Fantasies

Suicidal fantasies, often the first kind of suicidal thoughts that people have, are sometimes more concerned with the nonpersonal consequences of the suicidal act than with actually committing suicide. For example, some people fantasize about suicide not because they want to die, but because of the effect they think their death will have on others. Some people think about suicide as a means of punishing or getting even with someone. People also have suicidal fantasies that only concern themselves, with little or no regard for how their death or suicide will affect others. They fantasize about suicide as a means of removing themselves from a seemingly irresolvable crisis, an escape from an undesirable situation to a happier place or their desire to punish themselves for something they believe they have done wrong.

Suicidal Planning

As the idea of suicide as an effective problem-solving method takes root, a person may begin to focus more directly on how to achieve death, such as how, where and when he will attempt the act. He may approach this task eagerly and start looking for information on committing suicide, including reading books and talking with others who may be able to offer him ideas. He may also begin to obtain the means he needs to commit the suicidal act, such as a gun or potentially lethal drugs. He may also begin to get his affairs in order by tying up business matters, making a will and attending to other life-organizing tasks.

If the person has convinced himself that suicide is the best or only way to deal with his problems — if he has found "The Solution" — he may feel a new resolve. At this point, he may still be able to carry on or resume his normal daily activities.

In fact, with this new resolve, he may emerge from a depression and appear to be in a better frame of mind. Assessing individuals who are at this stage can be quite challenging because they often do not exhibit the overt signs that are commonly associated with suicidal behavior. In these cases, it can be helpful to consult other people who know the client to assist you in formulating an accurate assessment of risk.

Suicidal people sometimes become so completely consumed by their thoughts and plans for suicide that they think of little else. Their preoccupation takes precedence over everything except the most necessary thoughts and actions. It is not uncommon for people at this stage to become socially withdrawn to the point that they have difficulty maintaining any personal interactions and normal life activities. This isolation and social withdrawal are further compounded by a profound sense of depression and hopelessness. For those who have reached this stage, the risk for suicide is great.

COGNITIVE STYLE

Cognitive style refers to the way people organize their thinking, how they use this organizational scheme to approach life, and how that approach affects their view of themselves and the world in general. Cognitive style can be viewed as a mind-set that filters what a person sees and influences what he believes and how he acts. Once established, this mind-set is hard to change and can have far-reaching implications for many aspects of a person's life.

A good deal of research has been conducted on the ways in which suicidal people think. Some researchers have examined the idea that suicidal people seem to have distorted thought processes that affect their perceptions of themselves and the world around them and their decision-making and problem-solving abilities — all of which influence their risk for suicide. The cognitive process that contributes to suicidal thinking often starts with an irrational belief or a dysfunctional assumption that not only undermines a person's view of himself, but also affects his ability to solve problems and deal with daily life. Because he often sets up unrealistic goals for himself and because he tends to have poor problem-solving skills, his ability to reach these goals is limited. This in turn exposes him to a series of failures that create feelings of insecurity, inadequacy and self-doubt. The rigid, dichotomous nature of his thinking only serves to make matters worse by constricting and narrowing his options. With repeated unsuccessful attempts to solve their problems or fear that they won't be able to solve them, these people eventually come to feel that they will never be able to solve their problems or make their life situation better.

The Client's Ability to Communicate

Because a person's ability to communicate and understand information can provide clues about the way he thinks and processes information, these things are important to consider as part of every suicide assessment. For example, when people are in a situation that is causing them great emotional turmoil, they can become so overwhelmed that they are unable to organize their thinking in such a way that they can communicate their feelings. In the same way, they may find it difficult or impossible to process incoming information. They may also have difficulty understanding and communicating for reasons other than emotional turmoil. Perhaps the client has an illness that makes it difficult for him to hear or see or perhaps he has neurological problems. Maybe he is cognitively or mentally disorganized. Maybe he is so preoccupied and self-absorbed that he is simply unwilling or unable to talk to you. Of course, communication problems in and of themselves are by no means indications of heightened suicide risk, but they can be very useful to the big picture.

Dysfunctional Assumptions

Researchers (e.g., Ellis and Ratliff, 1986) have isolated several characteristic thinking patterns that may account for the cognitive differences between suicidal and nonsuicidal individuals. For lack of a more precise term, these thinking patterns have been labeled "dysfunctional assumptions." They are called dysfunctional because they are based on a variety of distorted beliefs and opinions that produce coping strategies that are counterproductive to effective functioning and problem-solving.

Irrational Beliefs

The first of these assumptions is referred to as irrational beliefs, which are discussed by cognitive theorists such as Albert Ellis (1962) and M.C. Maultsby (1975). Ellis' pioneering efforts were responsible for the development of a cognitive therapy approach called Rational-Emotive Therapy (RET) that stressed the relationships between thinking, emotions and actions. He asserted that emotional and behavioral responses are caused by a person's interpretation or perception of events rather than by the events themselves. In other words, it is not what happens to a person that causes him to react, but what the person thinks about what happened to him. Ellis proposed that emotional problems result when people attempt to live up to a set of convictions and personal expectations that are based on a belief system that is illogical, irrational and unobtainable.

The psychological consequences of having one's life governed by a set of irrational and illogical beliefs are enormous and can increase a person's risk for suicide. People who have a diminished self-esteem, who believe they are unworthy of being loved and socially undesirable can experience such overwhelming feelings of despair, loneliness and hopelessness that they may welcome suicide to escape the intense emotional pain. It is this type of irrational belief system that frequently dominates the thinking of people with a variety of psychological problems, including severe depression and suicidal preoccupation.

Dichotomous Thinking

Dichotomous thinking — the process of mentally categorizing life experiences into polar opposites — is a common cognitive error displayed by people with various psychological disorders as well as by people who are preoccupied with suicide. Often described as all-or-none thinking, dichotomous thinking means that a person sees the world in rigid terms. Things are either good or bad, right or wrong and there is seldom a middle ground or middle point of view. In terms of suicide assessment, determining that a client shows dichotomous thinking is not as important as determining how this kind of thinking affects him, especially in terms of how it interferes with interpersonal issues and the ability to find solutions to problems. The dichotomous thinker's inflexibility and cognitive rigidity significantly limit his creativity and hamper the development of new and potentially effective ideas and problem-solving approaches (Patsiokas et al., 1979).

Depressinogenic Attitudes

Depressinogenic attitudes are exhibited by individuals who possess an inherently negative, pessimistic perspective on life — seeing the glass half empty rather than half full. With a worldview that seldom recognizes, or even looks for, positive life events, these people rarely experience positive emotional feelings. They live with a constant level of unhappiness and dissatisfaction with everything and everyone. Consequently, they usually report greater levels of emotional distress and agitation and view life as more hopeless and futile with no expectation for positive change in the future. Not surprisingly, persons who are suicidal make these dysfunctional assumptions more often than those who are nonsuicidal. Ganzler (1967) writes that suicidal people may feel more negative about life than they are positive about death, that they are "being driven from life, into a state of non-being, which they designate as not being alive. At least on a semantic level, it is not so much that the suicidal person is pulled toward death as a positive, desired state as that he feels the need to remove himself from a painful and meaningless life."

Neurotic Perfectionism

Neurotic perfectionism, coined by Blatt (1995), is an irrational belief that has recently gained attention because of its relationship to suicidal thinking. Blatt argues that "normal" perfectionism (deriving satisfaction from painstaking efforts to excel and still being able to accept personal limitations) can sometimes be beneficial for personal motivation and achievement, while "neurotic" perfectionism (driven by an intense need to avoid failure) can be highly dysfunctional and lead to depression and thoughts of suicide. Blatt presents three basic types of perfectionism: other-oriented — involving the demand that others meet unrealistic standards; self-oriented — involving self-imposed unrealistic standards; and socially prescribed perfectionism — involving the belief that others are holding you to an unrealistic standard. The latter two types of perfectionism have been linked with a higher risk of depression and suicide.

People with neurotic perfectionism are always striving to

reach an unobtainable level of accomplishment. They always want to be perfect, to do everything right, never to be second best, always to have more, give more and do more. This desire often gives rise to intense feelings of fear, anxiety and inferiority because the individual is desperately trying to avoid failure, which is, of course, inevitable because no one is perfect. Because these individuals cannot live up to their own self-imposed expectations, they are caught in a never-ending cycle of self-defeating over-striving, leaving them feeling inferior, incompetent and unworthy of any of life's rewards.

Problem-Solving Deficiencies

Researchers have found various stylistic differences in the way suicidal and nonsuicidal, but depressed, patients approach problems, especially interpersonal problems. Schotte and Clum (1987), for example, found that suicidal patients initially had more difficulty figuring out how to label and attack a problem and even after they had identified the problem, they still had trouble generating and implementing a solution. And once they did generate a solution, they tended to focus primarily on the potentially negative outcomes. They were also deficient in their ability to figure out solutions to hypothetical interpersonal problems and they were less likely to anticipate the negative consequences of the solutions they chose.

Self-Perception

The way that a person perceives himself — his self-concept — may be an important variable in determining the likelihood that he will commit suicide. Because suicidal people generally have lower self-esteem than nonsuicidal people (Lester, 1992), clinicians should seek to determine how their client sees himself and, most importantly, why he feels the way he does. One study showed that many people who had committed suicide had a conflicted, unrealistic self-ideal (Richman and Eyman, 1990). Often, even though their personal goals far exceeded their abilities, they tried to attain perfection. Even though many of the subjects had low self-esteem, they were often very driven to achieve, but they set their sights on things they could not reach, causing them distress, feelings of failure and lowered self-esteem. This inability to reach unattainable goals also left them feeling bitter, empty, frustrated and full of rage (Smith and Eyman, 1988).

Other self-perceptions that have been reported in suicidal people include the presumed inability to control important aspects of their life and to initiate meaningful life changes, both of which are issues relating to self-competence — considered by some to be the basis of a person's sense of self-esteem. It is very difficult to hold yourself in high personal regard if you do not feel you are capable of mastering life's challenges. Farber (1968) said that for some people, the risk of suicide was increased because of a severely reduced sense of self-competence. When familiar ways of life are threatened, such people may become suicidal because they feel they cannot deal with the change. The lower the level of self-competence, the less serious the change needs to be to trigger these feelings.

There are a few simple methods that may help a clinician get a feel for the way a client perceives himself: (1) ask the client to describe himself, (2) give the client a list of adjectives and ask him to choose the words that best describe him, and (3) ask the client to suggest adjectives that describe how he would *like* to be and then compare the adjectives to the way he *actually* sees himself.

Hopelessness

Over the years, hopelessness has come to be considered one of the greatest correlates of suicidal preoccupation and behavior. Lester and co-workers (1975) reported that the subjects in their study who had more intent to die scored higher on a psychological measure of hopelessness, and in a follow-up study (1979) on the same group, the people who went on to kill themselves were among the most hopeless in the first study.

Future Orientation

One way to determine hopelessness is to explore how a client feels about his future. Many suicidal people think that death is a better alternative than living a life in which they believe there is no hope for a positive future. A client who feels very pessimistic and negative about his current life situation and cannot see any way to change that situation in the foreseeable future may understandably conclude that, for him, death is preferable to life. In fact, a negative expectation of the future and the resulting hopelessness that this creates has been found to be a better predictor of suicide than depression (Weishaar and Beck, 1992). This fact has been borne out repeatedly in suicide notes that reflect the futility and despair of completers who felt a pervasive sense of powerlessness to change their negative life situation.

On the other hand, even though one would think that a person's immediate plans for the future would suggest that he has reasons to continue living, this is not necessarily so. I have investigated many completed suicides in which the client had made plans to engage in future activities and he still committed suicide despite those plans. Therefore, although a potentially useful avenue to pursue during the assessment, the fact that a client has made plans to engage in some future activity is not always a reliable predictor of lowered suicide risk.

Beliefs about Suicide and Death

Because personal and cultural perceptions about suicide and death may affect a person's decision to commit suicide, clinicians should determine how the client feels about these subjects and how these attitudes may be influencing him. People perceive death in different ways. For example, some see it as an unknowable state, or as a state of oblivion, or as a continuance of life. Some believe that they will be reincarnated after death. Others see death as a way to be reunited with deceased loved ones. If any of these possibilities appeal to them, they may be encouraged to commit suicide. If any frighten them, they may decide that suicide is not for them. Furthermore, many people have cultural or philosophical biases about suicide. Particularly for religious reasons, some believe that it is not an acceptable practice and if they fear divine punishment, they may hesitate to kill themselves.

To determine a client's specific philosophical or religious views concerning death, clinicians can ask them to classify the concepts of life and death as positive or negative, ask them to agree or disagree with statements about death, and gauge their responses to words relating to death and suicide.

Having said all this, clinicians cannot assume that risk is lowered for clients with personal or cultural biases against suicide because a person who is determined to kill himself can always choose to abandon or modify his beliefs. A highly religious person, for example, may become an agnostic or an atheist if it allows him to find support for his desire to die. Or he may decide that God will understand his suffering and forgive him for committing suicide. Nevertheless, this may be helpful information, so clinicians should try to pursue these questions.

CHAPTER 7

Evaluation of Suicide Risk Potential

Now that we have completed the data collection phase of H.E.L.P.E.R. in which we identified all of the pertinent risk factors on the client, we turn to the important task of evaluating those data and deciding whether the client is at risk for suicide and if so, how much risk.

SUICIDE "PREDICTION"?

Before discussing the evaluation of suicide risk, we need to look at some very fundamental aspects of suicide assessment and at what practitioners realistically can and cannot do in terms of "predicting" suicide. First of all, the term "prediction" is very misleading because it suggests that there is some kind of magical element or prophecy involved in the endeavor. No one can predict another person's behavior with certainty and this is especially true with suicide. While we cannot say that a person will or will not try to kill himself, we can say that based on certain information, a person has a probability of attempting or not attempting suicide. In this way we can forecast the likelihood of suicidal behavior, but we cannot predict it.

In fact, to be perfectly honest, we cannot even forecast suicidal behavior with a great deal of certainty. This is because behavior does not always follow a set course and there are many reasons why a client may not act in a way that can be anticipated by the treating practitioner, despite how much he knows about the client. There is always the possibility that a person, especially one suffering from mental illness, will be influenced by irrational or illogical psychological factors that are difficult, if not impossible, to anticipate or predict. Also, when a client intentionally withholds vital information or gives false or misleading information, the clinician is further hampered in his ability to make an accurate assessment of suicide. This does not mean that we cannot or should not try to assess suicide risk; instead, my point here is that in some cases, it is not the practitioner's fault if he makes a mistake regarding risk due to inaccurate information provided by a dishonest or mentally ill client.

Moreover, suicide "predictions" are time-sensitive. This means that we cannot predict whether a person will or will not commit suicide next month or during his lifetime. Assessments are based on a combination of background conditions and current factors in a person's life, and the way in which they interact at a given time determines suicide risk. The moment those current factors change, the assessment is no longer valid. The bottom line is that the goal of a suicide assessment is not to predict suicide but to determine level of risk at a given time.

Suicide Assessment and Weather Forecasting

There are some interesting similarities between the way in which weather is predicted and the way in which certain behaviors, such as violence and suicide, are predicted or assessed. To help you understand some of the issues involved in "predicting" suicide, in the following discussion, I apply Monahan and Steadman's (1996) analogy between violence assessment and weather forecasting to suicide risk assessment.

Over the years, meteorologists have learned that certain weather conditions are associated with specific weather patterns. By analyzing these conditions and their various interactions, meteorologists provide daily forecasts of weather for different parts of the country — such as the likelihood of rain, storms or tornadoes. However, even though meteorologists know the conditions that lead to certain weather events, they still do not fully understand the precise interactions that cause a particular weather event to occur at a given moment in a given location. Until the event occurs, they can only estimate the likelihood of its occurrence, given the existing atmospheric conditions.

Of the basic strategies employed by meteorologists to forecast weather, the least used is the dichotomous method (e.g., It will be sunny today or it will be overcast today) because it is simply not accurate enough. If forecasters regularly relied on this kind of either/or approach, they would be wrong much of the time. To reduce the chance of error as much as possible, they often choose to play it safe by not offering a definitive forecast (It will be partly cloudy today). Unfortunately, while this nonspecific approach decreases the possibility of error, it is not very informative.

Probability estimates, the second and most familiar weather forecasting strategy used by meteorologists, are reported in terms of percentages (There will be a 30 percent chance of sunshine today). Even though probabilistic predictions seem to be a scientifically objective method of forecasting, they are actually very subjective. The data used to develop such predictions are collected, combined and analyzed according to the particular preferences of individual forecasters. As a result, even when the same data are used, probabilistic predictions may vary considerably from forecaster to forecaster. Another problem with probabilistic predictions is that these kinds of forecasts are often used incorrectly by the public or interpreted in a way other than they were meant. For example, some people may not consider a 40 percent chance of being hit by a hurricane as reason to evacuate their area, but they may be convinced by a 50 percent chance. In other words, the interpretation of these kinds of forecasts depends on each particular listener. In the case of rain showers, this may not be a serious problem, but in the case of a hurricane, it could be disastrous. This is one of the reasons why probabilistic estimates are not used for forecasting severe weather conditions that may involve the threat of major damage or loss of life. Another reason is because severe weather conditions such as hurricanes and tornadoes occur so infrequently that we do not have enough information about them to develop and refine reliable probability estimates.

Because of the drawbacks of using either dichotomous or probabilistic estimates for predicting severe weather conditions, most forecasters tend to prefer a categorical approach in which they use different categories of risk, such as watches and warnings, that they base on conditions known to be associated with severe weather. As the conditions increase in intensity, they issue stronger warnings. These predictions are often accompanied by information about additional actions (e.g., where to go in one's house in order to be safer) that may be taken in the event of particular conditions. Because it uses categories of risk based on known conditions, the categorical strategy is the preferred method for forecasting severe weather.

As you can see, forecasting the weather is similar in many ways to forecasting or assessing suicide. The similarity most pertinent to suicide assessment is the difficulty and inaccuracy of using either a dichotomous prediction strategy (He is suicidal/He is not suicidal) or a probabilistic prediction strategy (There is a 40 percent chance that he will kill himself). If you use either of these strategies, chances are good that your assessment will be wrong. Given the inadequacies of dichotomous and probabilistic prediction strategies, it probably makes the most sense to determine suicide risk using a categorical strategy.

SETTING TIME LIMITS TO SUICIDE ASSESSMENTS

Like severe weather forecasts, suicide assessments need to be based on current data and they are valid only as long as the situation stays the same. Therefore, in the event of a completed suicide, it is completely unrealistic for a clinician to be held responsible for an assessment that he conducted weeks or even months prior to the suicide. Indeed, a suicide assessor's accountability over time is an issue that few have been willing to address. Clearly, there are limits to the length of time a suicide assessment can be expected to be accurate, but that time period has never been established or even proposed by any professional organization. Unfortunately, because each case is different, it is impossible to propose a standard time limit that will have any degree of acceptance.

Meteorologists rarely make long-term forecasts and instead concentrate on forecasts that are directly related to current weather conditions because they know that the accuracy of their predictions decreases significantly as they extend beyond the immediate atmospheric conditions. Predictions extending past 12 to 24 hours show marked levels of inaccuracy and continue to deteriorate steadily. For this reason, meteorologists will rarely forecast next week's weather, much less next month's. And, in the event of severe weather, they sometimes update their forecasts hourly to ensure that they are taking advantage of the most current data.

This does not mean that clinicians cannot use the same type of method as weather forecasters do to establish reasonable parameters within which their assessment results can be used. They should, in fact, state in their documentation of the case that their decision is based on risk factors that are associated with *current* conditions in the client's life and that the estimation of risk potential will hold true for as long as the current conditions remain the same. Risk determinations should not last for an undefined period of time, but rather should be directly tied to the existence of specific risk factors. As the factors change and as risks become higher or lower, the assessment will change accordingly. By applying a time limit to your assessment of a client's risk for suicide, you will be able to present a more accurate and realistic clinical picture, and in the event of a completed suicide, you will be better able to defend yourself in court.

ASSIGNING RISK TO YOUR CLIENT'S BEHAVIOR

The clinician's goal at this point of the assessment is to determine the client's level of suicide risk based on the information he has gathered. Suicidal behavior occurs along a continuum that can range from noninjurious (no risk) to highly lethal (extreme risk), and the goal of this part of the assessment is to determine where the client lies on the continuum at this particular point in time. While there will always be exceptions to this concept, I think it is safe to say that people will not usually be at the high-risk end of the continuum without first having passed through at least some of the earlier, less lethal stages. You have to keep in mind, however, that this concept must be applied with the clear understanding that the relationship between lethality and each category of risk is not empirically derived and cannot be used definitively to establish risk. The behavior of suicide is not so much a result of which specific risk factors a person has, but how those risk factors come together in a certain way and at a certain point in time to reach the point of suicide. Therefore, while the categories listed below can help you to make systematic decisions about a client's level of risk for suicide that are logical and defensible, they must be considered in terms of each client's unique situation.

No Risk to Minimal Risk

People who are at the lowest level of suicide risk — no risk to minimal risk — show no apparent risk factors and there is no reason to assume they are going to kill themselves at this point in time. In most cases, they have not harmed themselves in any way, nor do they have any desire to. People who are at minimal risk may have vague ideation of death and/or suicide and they may have verbalized these thoughts. However, before determining that a client with even minimal suicidal ideation is not at risk, you should make specific inquiries about the motivation for his suicidal thoughts.

Low Risk

People at the second level — a low risk potential for suicide — may have engaged in self-destructive behavior, but usually without suicidal intent, and it is usually of minimal lethality. This category may include people who have engaged in acts of self-harm for manipulative reasons or to call attention to their pain or their need for help. Self-mutilators who have no interest in killing themselves, especially those who engage in the behavior chronically, may also fall into this category. They may present with a family history of dysfunction, a recent devastating loss or other current stressor, and a history of depression or drug abuse.

Moderate Risk

The third level — moderate risk — includes people who have engaged in self-destructive behavior without suicidal intent but with moderate to high lethality and people with suicidal intent whose attempts have been of low lethality. Individuals at moderate risk may have a family history of major dysfunction, including parents with psychiatric disorders and substance abuse problems who may have attempted or completed suicide. These clients may have suffered physical and/or emotional abuse. They may also have a psychiatric diagnosis, recent stressors, a lack of support systems, easy access to lethal means and a crude suicide plan.

High to Extreme Risk

Individuals who are at a high to extreme risk for suicide have usually engaged in self-destructive behavior with serious suicidal intent and moderate to high lethality or have engaged in less lethal behavior but have ongoing suicidal intent. For people at this level, many risk factors have come together to form a volatile cluster. These risk factors could include a history of chronic suicide attempts with increasing lethality and intent, a history of psychiatric illness, especially schizophrenia and bipolar disorders, significant levels of internal or external stress, progressive isolation from family and friends, and an accelerated effort to develop an effective suicide plan.

ESTIMATING RISK

To estimate risk, the clinician must review each of the H.E.L.P.E.R. components to determine which risk factors are present, the level or degree of those factors, their unique interaction, and the extent to which the client's statements and behavior support or refute any collateral material.

The clinician can make an initial estimate of risk by determining which risk category corresponds to the unique mixture of risk characteristics exhibited by the client. Once the clinician has accounted for each of the H.E.L.P.E.R. components and refined the estimate by comparing them, he must then report his risk estimate, which we will discuss in the next chapter.

Overestimating Risk: Why You Should Not Do It

Because of the legal ramifications of underestimating a client's risk for suicide, some practitioners may feel a need to protect themselves by reporting that their clients are suicidal, whether they actually are or not. They apparently think that it is better to incorrectly diagnose someone as suicidal than risk a legal confrontation if a suicide death occurs. Although this kind of thinking is understandable, it is not clinically or professionally sound. If you assess nonsuicidal clients as suicidal, everyone suffers, including yourself.

First, the client suffers in that he may receive inappropriate treatment. If you indicate that a client is a very high risk for suicide, treatment recommendations will have to correspond with this diagnosis. This becomes especially serious when psychiatric hospitalization or medications are recommended. Second, if the practitioners responsible for diagnosing the behavior make no distinction between their suicidal and nonsuicidal clients, practitioners who work with these clients in the future will have a distorted understanding of their history. Third, if you continually identify all of your clients as suicidal, eventually it will come back to haunt you. After a while, the professional skills of a clinician who has had nothing but high-risk clients will become suspect.

In terms of your own legal protection, it may be argued that

extreme caution is the safest approach when predicting suicide risk, but to knowingly overdiagnose suicidality simply
for your own protection is unethical and clearly unfair to the
client. If you can determine with a high degree of certainty
that an individual does not intend to kill himself — that he is,
for example, displaying suicidal-like behavior for manipulative reasons — then you should most definitely make this distinction. This is not an easy call and the repercussions of
being wrong are potentially severe, but if you follow the
H.E.L.P.E.R. system, you should have all of the information
you need to make accurate diagnoses — and at the same time
be able to support your diagnosis with hard data that will
protect you legally.

PEER CONSULTATION

Mental health practitioners often overlook, or chose not to
use, an extremely valuable resource that is always available to
them — the opinions of their colleagues. As a result, they frequently make very difficult, extremely complex and potentially life-threatening decisions in a vacuum. The reasons that
practitioners do not get second opinions are varied, but whatever the reason, it is a bad mistake. Peer consultation can be
one of the most important clinical and legal safeguards a
practitioner has at his disposal, especially when dealing with
clients whose cases are ambiguous. To ignore this resource
can expose you and your clients to needless risk.

Peer consultation is not necessary in all cases, but in those
instances where you are uncertain about ambiguous issues, it
can be a valuable tool to either validate or challenge your
ideas and assumptions. Another clinician's opinion may also
uncover important information. Of course, consulting a colleague does not absolve you of primary responsibility for any
decisions you ultimately make, nor does it require you to alter

your initial opinions. It is to your advantage, both clinically and legally, to consult with peers. Not only does it show that you care enough about the case to seek another opinion, but also that you exercised reasonable and prudent judgment.

FOLLOW-UP EVALUATION

Because suicidal intention is a dynamic process, it is important to re-evaluate the client's risk potential. This means having periodic contact with clients who pose a suicide threat until the level of risk is deemed to be minimal. The amount and quality of contact typically is left to the discretion of each practitioner, but higher levels of risk usually require more frequent (sometimes even daily) contact, while for lower-risk clients, it will be less often. Because the nature and frequency of follow-up contacts is discretionary (unless prescribed by a specific operational policy of an organization or agency), it is important for practitioners to be able to provide a rationale for their follow-up arrangements.

CHAPTER 8

Reporting Risk: The Documentation Process

In this final step — a most critical part of the assessment process — you will write a report that formally documents your evaluation of the client's current risk for suicide (i.e., his risk at the time of the interview). This documentation should not only present your estimation of risk, it should also provide a thorough explanation of how and why you arrived at this determination. Great care should be taken to clearly explain the logic behind your conclusions and every effort should be made to support your statements with facts. Your report should demonstrate that you conducted a complete assessment that explored all the factors that could potentially impact on the client's suicidality (or lack thereof). Writing this report is a complicated and challenging undertaking, but it will serve you well to take your time and write a report that meets its goals of being both an accurate, thorough and informative clinical document that will assist practitioners who subsequently treat the client and, as we will discuss below, a document that will safeguard you in the event that legal action is brought against you.

LEGAL ASPECTS OF DOCUMENTATION

While providing documentation about observations and treatment of a client is a typical part of every health care provider's job, when the client involved is potentially suicidal, this documentation assumes a much greater significance, not so much in terms of its clinical utility, but in terms of its *legal* utility. In the event that a client commits suicide and litigation is brought against you as his mental health care provider, your report is really the only hard evidence that exists of your interaction with the client and your role in his case. It is the only "official" record of your assessment of his risk for suicide and your recommendations for treatment or any interventions you may have suggested and/or implemented. Not only will a clinician's determination of a client's suicide risk be investigated, but so will the processes and methods he used to reach it. In fact, for the court, the central legal question is not whether the practitioner was right or wrong in his assessment of risk but whether he arrived at his determination logically, using accepted professional procedures.

The report often becomes the central focus of the trial, and both sides — your defense counsel and the plaintiff's counsel — will use it to try to win the case. You will use the report to defend your actions and decisions, and the opposing counsel will try to use it against you to challenge your decisions and show that you did something wrong. (Furthermore, if the case does not go to court for a long time, as often happens, thorough and detailed documentation will help you remember the details of the case. Practitioners often see hundreds of clients a year and it is hardly a poor reflection of your memory or interest in your clients if, after time has elapsed, you cannot remember every detail of every case.)

Because few reports undergo as intense a level of scrutiny as suicide assessment reports undergo in the courtroom, it is imperative for you to be extremely careful about what you write and how you write it. You should make every effort to communicate clearly and avoid wording that could be misinterpreted. The information you include should be accurate, informative and, above all, your conclusions and decisions have to be defensible in every way. Make sure that your report meets these standards while you are writing it, not while you are being cross-examined by the plaintiff's lawyer. In fact, as Gutheil (1980) wrote in a well-known paper, you should write your report as if a lawyer were sitting on your shoulders, reviewing every word. The suggestions discussed below will not only protect you in the courtroom, but they will also strengthen the clinical utility of your report.

The fact that this documentation can become the basis of legal action against practitioners is a reality that they must accept and must be prepared to deal with. Those who ignore this basic fact are needlessly putting themselves in jeopardy. And, contrary to common belief, protecting yourself legally should not in any way interfere with good clinical practice. The two can and should go hand in hand. The emotional, professional and financial costs of losing a lawsuit can be devastating, but they will be even harder to accept if they occur because you didn't write your report properly.

Think Ahead: Pay Attention to the Readers of Your Report

One of the most effective ways to write a suicide assessment report is to remind yourself that you are trying to communicate information to other people. Even though you may end up being the only person who ever reads this documentation, you should always think ahead and automatically assume that others *will* read it — not only other practitioners who may treat the client in the future, but those who are involved in bringing litigation against you or those defending you. If you think this way, it will help you to see your report as others will and this will encourage you to assess it objectively. As you write, challenge the assumptions and determinations that you've made about the client and his potential for suicide. Re-examine your conclusions to test the logic of your decisions. You should also ask yourself the following kinds of questions:

- ❑ Have I given enough information to support my findings?
- ❑ Are my findings supported by facts rather than assumptions?
- ❑ Will others understand what I have written?
- ❑ Have I presented the information in a logical format?
- ❑ Can anything I've said be misinterpreted?
- ❑ Can anything I've said be used against me or placed in a negative context?

Finally, the process of writing this report will help you clarify the thinking behind your estimation of the client's risk for suicide and your suggestions for intervention or treatment. Often, when you put your thoughts down on paper, it allows you to see things more clearly and in a different light. You should use the writing of your report as a means of thinking your thoughts through, testing and refining your logic, and exploring possible alternative estimates of risk or methods of treatment. In this way, you can use your record-keeping as a framework for organizing your decision-making.

Also, because there is a good chance that your report will be reviewed by those who may be less familiar with suicide and suicide assessment procedures than yourself, it is in your best interest to express yourself in straightforward, nontechnical and jargon-free terms. You do not want to open the door for misinterpretation, confusion and unintended inferences. After putting your report through these tests, you should feel confident that you have made the right clinical decisions and expressed them in such a way that others will understand your thinking.

Presenting Your Findings: How Much Information Should You Include?

There is a fine line between providing sufficient information and superfluous information and you must try to find that balance. From a legal perspective, it may be dangerous to say too much and it may be dangerous to say too little. If you write a long report — say 25 pages — as I have known colleagues to do, you are probably including more information than is clinically relevant and you may be giving opposing counsel too much ammunition to attack you with. The more information you give, the greater the chances that opposing counsel will be able to find conflicts, inconsistencies or issues to challenge your assessment procedures and conclusions. An overly long report filled with too many unnecessary details may not bear directly on the quality or accuracy of your assessment, but the confusion and negative impressions it can leave in the minds of jurors can have disastrous consequences. Furthermore, when you offer too much information, you may run the risk of clouding important clinical issues with unnecessary detail. This does not mean, however, that you should not provide thorough and detailed documentation. When you do, it indicates a high standard of care, shows your concern as a practitioner and reflects your professionalism to those reading your report. At the other extreme, a report that is too short and contains minimal or abbreviated information may not only imply that you have conducted a very limited or incomplete assessment, it could also be seen as showing a lack of concern for the client's situation. Moreover, it could be seen as plain carelessness. Reports that are overly long or too short reflect poorly on your performance, perhaps suggesting that you were as careless with your assessment as you were with your documentation. The bottom line is that you need to strike a balance between saying too much and saying too little while adequately communicating all of the necessary information.

Be Objective: Rely on Facts, Not Conjecture

While clinical judgment is an integral part of every suicide assessment, if your report relies heavily on your subjective opinions or feelings about the client, you can find yourself in serious trouble in the courtroom (not to mention increasing your chances of *ending up* in the courtroom). One of the goals stressed throughout this book — and a main source of legal protection — is basing your estimation of the client's risk for suicide on actual facts rather than on speculation, assumptions or your personal ideas and beliefs. Relying heavily on subjective opinion is never a good idea — either while conducting your assessment or while writing your report. Not only are personal opinions much easier to dispute than facts, but an assessment based on opinion can give the impression that your report is nothing more than speculation based on your personal beliefs. Similarly, you should avoid using theoretical concepts to support your conclusions because they are often subject to a wide range of conflicting interpretations.

Throughout the report, whenever you need to state your opinion — and of course you will — you should always try to support it with facts that reinforce your conclusions. It may be helpful to quote some of the client's important statements verbatim. Whenever possible, you should try to let the facts make your point for you. This is an effective way of showing that your reasoning flows directly from a factual source. Finally, you should always avoid making judgmental, negative or derogatory comments about your clients because it gives the appearance of bias and can easily be interpreted as unprofessional.

Check Your Facts: Accuracy Reflects on Professionalism

While lack of attention to details may not have anything to do with the overall value or accuracy of your assessment, it can give the impression that you were as careless with your data collection and your evaluation of the client's risk as you were with your report. It is therefore essential that all of the data cited in your report are accurate. For instance, make sure that you have included the correct dates, times and places of important events such as prior suicide attempts, psychiatric hospitalizations and recent incidents that may have influenced the client's potential for suicide. Also, if there were any important contradictions that emerged during the course of the assessment, make sure to point them out and discuss their relevance. For example, if your client told you that he was seriously intent on dying and that he took a massive overdose of sleeping pills that nearly killed him, but hospital records indicate that he ingested only 10 aspirin tablets, which did him no harm, you should indicate this contradiction and its significance in your report. Finally, it is critical to proofread your report for misspellings, poor grammar, incorrect punctuation and awkward wording of sentences. This may seem unimportant, but these kinds of errors give a very bad impression and reflect poorly on your professionalism.

Altering Your Reports: Never Do It!

Tampering with your report after a client commits suicide is absolutely one of the greatest mistakes you can make. If additional information comes to your attention after a completed suicide or if you realize that you have forgotten to include relevant information, document the information in an addendum to the original report, clearly noting the date of the addition. If there is any indication that you have altered, deleted or added information to your original report after a suicide, it can raise serious questions about the accuracy and veracity of your report, not to mention your integrity as a practitioner. Several years ago in a malpractice suit filed by the relatives of a man who had committed suicide, the plaintiffs alleged that the client's death resulted from the fact that the practitioner did not refer the client for additional help or recommend hospitalization. The practitioner contended that he *had* made a referral — after all, he claimed, he had noted it in his report. The only thing he said he *hadn't* done was to make sure that the client followed through with his suggestion. The plaintiffs hired a document analyst who was able to convince the jury that the referral mentioned in the assessment report was added *after* the client's suicide. They won a settlement of $580,000. Clearly, severe legal problems can arise if you give any reason for others to believe that you have falsified or changed your report in any way. If there is any indication that you falsified your report, the assumption will be that you made a mistake, that you knew it and that you tried to hide the error. In almost all cases, it is better to admit errors than to alter your report to hide them.

THE ASSESSMENT REPORT: WHAT TO INCLUDE AND HOW TO ORGANIZE IT

The following is only a suggested format for writing your report. You will probably find that you will need to expand, modify or delete some of the headings listed below to make them suit the circumstances of each individual case. Of course, subjects that don't have any relevance to your client should be omitted except in cases where the *lack* of a risk factor acts as a protective element against suicide, or when a risk factor has the opposite of the expected effect. Feel free to combine sections and move them around according to the kinds of points you want to make and the client's particular situation. To avoid repetition of material and a diluted presentation, you may find that the best way to report your findings is to use only a few main headings. However, you can still use the following suggested sections as a guide for what to include.

Basic Information

Give the client's full name, age, gender and race/ethnic group. Indicate the date, location and length of the interview. Indicate the extent of previous contact with the client, if any.

Reason for the Assessment

Indicate how the client came to be assessed (e.g., referral, walk-in clinic, emergency room admission). If it was the result of a referral, give the date, the name of the referring party and any specific referral questions that were asked.

Sources of Information

You should reference the sources of information that you used during your assessment (documents, interviews with other parties, etc.) This list should be detailed enough to permit subsequent follow-up (e.g., "I reviewed the client's inpatient records from his admission to Presbyterian Hospital on November 15, 1999 and spoke with his doctor of record, Samuel Webster, MD").

Physical Appearance and Behavioral Observations

Present a complete and objective description of the client's overall demeanor, including his physical appearance (hygiene, grooming, manner of dress) and his overt behavior (posture, body language, etc.) and general emotional state (depressed, hysterical). You should also discuss the client's ability and desire to communicate with you and his general approach and reactions to the interview. Indicate his degree of openness with you, his cooperation during the interview and his ability to understand your questions. Describe his reactions to important topics of discussion.

Historical Factors

Personal History

Clearly identify and describe any events or experiences in the client's past that have been associated with suicide, specifically a history of psychiatric disorders (including alcohol and/or substance abuse) and past suicide attempts. If the client has received treatment for any mental disorders, make sure to give the specifics (type, length, dates and place of treatment) as well as the client's response and perceptions of the treatment. Because the similarity of current behavior to past behavior will strengthen your estimate of risk, you should try to associate current findings with previous difficulties the client may have had, noting consistencies and discrepancies.

Starting with the most recent incidents and working backwards, describe in detail any self-destructive behavior, especially suicide attempts that had a high level of intent and lethality. You should also describe any suicidal thoughts that the client may have had that he didn't act on. Aside from basic statistics (number and dates of incidents), be sure to include the causal factors, the methods used, the consequences, and in the case of suicide attempts, why they failed. Indicate whether a pattern exists in the client's methods and motives, and any lessons that he may have learned from these attempts.

Family History

Document any information about family members who have committed or attempted suicide or who have experienced mental health problems or hospitalization for psychiatric problems. Indicate the client's relationship with the family member(s) who has committed or attempted suicide and state what he feels about the behavior and what he may have learned from these incidents. Indicate any dysfunctional events in the client's family life that have been associated with completed suicide, including drug/alcohol abuse, physical and emotional abuse, divorce, conflict and stress, and the degree of dysfunctional problem-solving skills the client may have learned from his family.

Environmental Factors

Demographic Factors

Here you have the opportunity to strengthen your case by comparing the client's demographic profile to the statistics on individuals who have committed suicide, including gender, age, race, marital status, illness and unemployment. If your client falls into one of the high-risk demographic groups (elderly, adolescent, young black males, etc.), you should expand on these areas, describing the particular factors that increase risk in these groups.

Life Events and Life Circumstances

Here you will describe issues relating to the client's current life situation, paying special attention to circumstances that have been associated with completed suicide, such as a lack of employment, illness, divorce, separation or widowhood. Include a description of his current living situation. Does the live alone? Is he incarcerated, in a nursing home, in a hospital? If there are events that are currently causing him high levels of stress, explain what these stressors are and how they are affecting him, paying particular attention to events that research has shown to have precipitated or preceded suicide. Describe any recent losses the client may have suffered — whether they are real or perceived — including the loss of a loved one to death or separation, the threatened loss of a lover or other significant relationship, the loss of a job or a home, loss of freedom, and the loss of health or physical ability because of sickness or injury. There is also emotional or psychological loss, such as loss of identity, self-esteem or personal respect. If the client has suffered stressors such as legal problems, scandals or other humiliating events that are causing him severe distress, describe them and their impact on him.

Support Systems

Because lack of a support system can act as a risk factor for suicide, indicate the existence and quality of the client's social support systems. Indicate what kind of support it is (personal support from friends and family or institutional support from agencies, treatment providers or social service organizations). Also indicate the degree to which the client perceives support to be available and is willing to make use of it.

Lethality

This part of the report, one of the most important sections, is where you indicate the client's actual chances of dying from his self-destructive behavior. If the client has recently engaged in an act of self-destruction or if he has had ideation about or has verbalized thoughts of suicide, you should describe these things carefully, incorporating the following components into your discussion.

Intent to Die

It is critically important to address the client's intent to die because it bears so directly on his potential for death. Indicate whether he has recently engaged in a physical act of self-harm or verbalized, threatened or had ideation about death and/or suicide and discuss the seriousness, intensity or degree of sincerity of his intent to die. (Even though you may have already mentioned the client's past self-destructive behavior in the history section, you may find it helpful to describe it here too, because past behavior may be a very good predictor of future behavior.) Pay particular attention to the client's motivation for current self-destructive behaviors and thoughts. Is he seriously intent on killing himself or is he engaging in them for reasons of manipulation, self-mutilation, or as a cry for help? Always try to support your estimation of the client's intent with hard facts. For example, if he has written a suicide note, engaged in life-organizing behaviors or given away cherished possessions, be sure to include this information.

Suicide Plan

Because having a suicide plan is a strong indication of increased intent — and if the plan is a good one, his chances of dying are increased — you should offer thorough and detailed documentation about it. Some of the important aspects of the client's plan that you should address include the following:

- ❑ the extent of planning he has done
- ❑ the level of organization of the plan

❑   the effectiveness of the plan
❑   his choice of method
❑   the physical dangerousness of the chosen method
❑   the extent to which his choice of means is consistent
    with his desire to die
❑   his ability to access the chosen means
❑   his knowledge of using the means or method
❑   the extent to which he has attempted to obtain a
    means of death
❑   the extent to which he has made efforts to avoid
    discovery or rescue
❑   the extent to which access can be limited or con-
    trolled

Access to and Knowledge of Means

If the client does not have a plan but his environment offers
him particularly easy access to or special knowledge about
using lethal means, you may want to describe this here (e.g.,
a policeman who owns a gun or an adolescent whose father
has a gun collection). You may also want to include in this
section documentation about clients who, although lacking a
plan, have made a special effort to find out information about
methods of committing suicide.

Psychological Factors

This section should be used to discuss relevant aspects of the
client's psychiatric history, his suicidal ideation as indicated
by his verbal statements (and information from collateral
sources) and the overall cognitive style he uses to solve problems and cope with the internal and external pressures he is
experiencing.

Psychiatric Disorders

Discuss in detail the client's current psychiatric status, carefully documenting psychiatric disorders that have been associated with completed suicide (e.g., mood disorders, depression, schizophrenia and borderline personality disorder). It is also important to document any alcohol or drug abuse. Try to support your discussion with hard fact and information from collateral sources, including whether the client has been hospitalized, any psychiatric records that you may have consulted and information from the client's family or other close associates.

Aside from indicating that risk is increased by the mere existence of psychiatric disorders and substance abuse problems, you should show how they may be influencing the client's frame of mind and lifestyle and whether these in turn have increased his risk for suicide. If the client was intoxicated at the time of the interview, it is important to indicate this and explain how it may have affected your assessment of risk. If you had to re-interview the client or, even more importantly, feel you *need* to, make sure to document this in your report.

Suicidal Ideation

This section, a very important part of the report, should include information about the presence and seriousness of the client's suicidal thinking. Indicate whether the information you obtained is from the direct or indirect verbal statements made by the client or from other sources. If the client has been thinking about suicide or death, you should indicate the motivation for the thoughts and whether the ideation consists of active thoughts of suicide or a passive desire for death. Also, indicate the frequency, duration and intensity of his suicidal thoughts. If the client has told you specifically that he is suicidal or that he is not, you should document this and indicate your assessment of the truthfulness of this statement and your reasons for making this determination.

Cognitive Style

In this section, you should focus on identifying the client's predominant thinking styles and the way they affect his self-perception and his ability to solve problems. It is important to address the presence of any dysfunctional assumptions and attitudes, dichotomous and rigid thinking, and persistence in adhering to ineffective problem-solving strategies. The presence of hopelessness, one of the major risk factors for suicide, should be carefully documented.

Evaluation of Risk Potential

Here you should make a clear and definitive statement about your assessment of the client's risk for suicide at the time of your interview. It can be beneficial to begin this section with a standard statement that orients the reader to the parameters of the report's conclusions and suicide assessments in general (i.e., that we cannot actually predict suicide with certainty and that suicide assessments are time-limited).

Treatment Recommendations

We do not cover treatment issues in this book, but because it is usually an integral part of documentation, some information regarding treatment recommendations may be helpful.

Begin with a brief summary of the case and your findings. Restate the client's name, the referral source and the circumstances surrounding the referral. Restate in clear terms the level of risk that currently exists and, in abbreviated form, the specific results and conclusions that led to that finding. It may be appropriate at this point to provide a brief explanation of the logic you employed in linking the data with the level of risk.

Treatment or management recommendations should be as specific as possible, leaving as little room as possible for misinterpretation or confusion. It may be valuable to explore the range of options available for the client and to establish a strategy based on those options. It is also important to provide a brief rationale for the actions you have recommended. It may be beneficial to address how the treatment plan will be implemented and whether follow-up procedures will be necessary.

CHAPTER 9

Legal Issues Involved in Suicide Litigation

In the mental health service professions, the number of cases involving malpractice litigation has skyrocketed over the last 20 years. Prior to the 1960s, lawsuits against mental health professionals were relatively rare and when they were brought, the defending practitioner usually won (Robertson, 1988). In a review of the literature from 1946 through 1961, Bellamy (1962) found only 18 cases where mental health professionals were found liable in malpractice suits. However, this relaxed legal climate soon changed. Data reported for the period 1976 to 1986 by the American Psychological Association Insurance Trust indicate that over 1,000 persons filed malpractice suits. More recently, a review of psychiatric malpractice cases (Robertson, 1988) found that suits involving suicide accounted for 21 percent of the claims filed between 1980 and 1985. Not only has the number of malpractice suits increased consistently in recent years, the financial awards have also increased, with claims of one million dollars being commonplace. Furthermore, failure to prevent suicide has become one of the leading causes for malpractice suits against mental health professionals. As a result, it would seem to be in the best interests of mental health service providers to accept this reality and become more aware of their legal vulnerabilities.

Operating from the premise that what you don't know about the law can definitely hurt you, this chapter provides a brief overview of the basic legal criteria and standards of performance associated with suicide litigation. When we speak of legal criteria, we are referring to the legal standards that have been established by the courts to protect patients by ensuring that practitioners provide them with adequate clinical treatment. The fundamental legal standard of care for mental health practitioners is that once a practitioner-client relationship has been established, the clinician has a legal responsibility to offer reasonable and adequate care to that client. This is referred to as a "minimum standard of care." Even though most practitioners would like to think that they provide more than an adequate or minimum standard of care, for your own legal safety, it is essential to know what the law considers the standard of care.

It is important for health care providers to be aware of the fact that the merits of a particular case do not matter; any clinician can be named in a lawsuit regardless of his conduct. While the legal profession makes every effort to limit and, in obvious cases, impose sanctions on attorneys who file frivolous lawsuits, they can and do occur. In some cases, the issues alleged in a lawsuit simply reflect legitimate differences of opinion between sides. For these and other reasons, being sued is not an indication, and certainly not proof, of wrongdoing and it should never be construed as such. In light of the emotional and financial costs involved in suffering through the ordeal of a lawsuit, even winning can be a hollow victory for the prevailing practitioner. Therefore, the best way to protect yourself is not only to conduct suicide assessments that conform to the legal standards, but also to know the basic legal elements involved in suicide litigation.

BASIC TYPES OF LEGAL LIABILITY

Most lawsuits brought against practitioners are tort actions — a general class of lawsuits that are filed against anyone who has allegedly caused harm to others. Tort actions are civil actions, in other words, they are not criminal cases in which the defendant, if found guilty, may receive a term of imprisonment. Civil actions are nothing more than a way for one individual to obtain redress for a wrong caused by the negligent or intentional acts of another. In civil actions, plaintiffs have to provide a lower standard of proof to support their claim than they have to provide in criminal cases. Civil cases typically require only a preponderance of the evidence, which is usually understood to mean at least a 51 percent certainty of guilt. Criminal cases require proof of guilt beyond a reasonable doubt. While some cases involve both civil and criminal penalties, most tort actions do not involve criminal sanctions, and instead tend to result in monetary awards as compensation for the wrongdoing or for the loss suffered.

There are three basic types of tort actions that mental health services providers should be familiar with: negligence, malpractice and deliberate indifference. Each of these actions is similar and to some degree related, but they typically arise from different circumstances and mean different things in the courtroom. They also require different legal tests and levels of proof to determine liability.

Negligence

Negligence, the simplest tort action, is nothing more than the failure of a person to act in a reasonable and prudent manner. Any person may be sued in a tort action for negligence and the basic test is what a reasonable and prudent person would do under similar circumstances. Negligence suits typically do not pertain directly to professional conduct, but to a wider range of actions that result in damage to the client. For most health care practitioners, simple negligence claims arise from their failure to follow prescribed policies, procedures and protocols. In institutional settings where care is provided according to set policies or procedures, any violation of these practices may be seen as negligence. Practitioners at all levels of the organization will be held accountable for any deviation they make from that policy, regardless of their reason for not meeting the requirements. The basic assumption in these types of cases is relatively straightforward — that reasonable and prudent practitioners do not fail to conform to established institutional policy.

Malpractice

Malpractice is a type of tort action that is filed against a professional person for not exercising reasonable and prudent actions in the delivery of a specialized service. In other words, malpractice can be seen as a form of professional negligence. More precisely, malpractice can be defined as the failure of a professional to treat a client with the same degree of reasonable care and skill usually exercised by similar professionals who are in good standing in their profession. We will discuss the specific criteria involved in malpractice litigation more thoroughly in the section covering the components of malpractice.

Deliberate Indifference

Deliberate indifference is a far more serious breach of conduct than either negligence or malpractice and brings into question constitutional issues involving the civil rights of the plaintiff. Deliberate indifference cases seek to show that persons who are responsible for providing or overseeing services to residents of facilities or institutional settings (such as prisons or hospitals where individuals often reside without choice) have ignored or disregarded the inadequate delivery of those services. They emanate from Eighth Amendment protection against cruel and unusual punishment in the case of criminal defendants, or Fourteenth Amendment safeguards regarding the right to due process in the case of those involuntarily held without conviction.

Courts have ruled that simple negligence or malpractice alone does not constitute a constitutional violation. In comparison, deliberate indifference requires that administrators or clinicians intentionally delayed care, denied appropriate care or were callously indifferent to an obvious need for care. This standard requires the plaintiff to demonstrate a clear pattern of neglect, intent to inflict injury or suffering, or to show that the defendant intentionally and knowingly departed from accepted professional practice. A finding of deliberate indifference requires proof that the professional who is responsible for the services, in a willful, mean-spirited and callous manner, sought to deliberately deprive an individual of his basic right to necessary and needed treatment. A defendant found to have been deliberately indifferent can be liable for punitive damages, payment of all attorney fees, or in extreme cases, criminal sanctions. Given the severity of the penalties involved, the evidence in these cases must be substantial and the burden of proof rests entirely with the plaintiff.

Although in some instances the concepts of negligence, malpractice and deliberate indifference may overlap, in most cases, the legal test for deliberate indifference is so rigorous that it is usually not raised, except under the most egregious conditions. Nevertheless, considering the gravity of the issues and the potential consequences for adverse findings, those responsible for conducting suicide assessments, treatment or prevention programs should understand their liability and the potential repercussions if their program services are being provided inadequately, particularly when they are aware of such problems.

THE COMPONENTS OF MALPRACTICE

For the remainder of the chapter we will focus mainly on issues related to clinical malpractice because this is the type of suit that is most often brought against mental health providers. It is essential for clinicians to know the specific criteria and tests that are used to determine the validity of malpractice complaints. Even though practitioners often use the terms negligence and malpractice, many of them don't really know what they mean. This self-perceived level of knowledge can create a false sense of security that will crumble as soon as they are confronted with an actual legal challenge. Fortunately, the basic legal criteria for these actions are relatively easy to understand and the standards for proving them are more rigorous than most practitioners realize. In fact, given the difficulty of proving malpractice, it can be argued that the fear of losing a lawsuit far exceeds the actual threat. Nevertheless, for anyone who deals with potentially suicidal individuals, even the *threat* of litigation is a serious concern.

By understanding the legal guidelines and procedures used to assess the merits of a malpractice claim, practitioners will know how to conform to legal standards. We will also concentrate on the requirements for establishing a malpractice claim and the way in which legal standards are typically determined in the courtroom, particularly through the use of expert witnesses.

To sustain a claim of malpractice, a plaintiff must prove, by a preponderance of the evidence, the existence of four key elements:

1. A relationship existed that creates a duty
2. Professional conduct was below an accepted standard
3. The patient was actually harmed
4. The professional's conduct caused harm

A quick way to remember these four essential elements is with the following mnemonic device called the "Four D's" — **D**ereliction of **D**uty that **D**irectly causes **D**amage (Bongar, 1992, credits Sadoff, cited in Rachlin, 1984). A clinician can use this rule of thumb to assess the likelihood of a plaintiff's success in establishing a malpractice claim.

Creating a Duty

When applied to malpractice, this concept assumes that a "special relationship" has been created between two individuals in which one person has agreed to provide some level of care, supervision or assistance for the other. It involves the creation of a contract between the professional and the client and implies some degree of obligation on the part of the professional to provide care. This obligation or contract does not depend on receiving payment for service, but rather on the "reasonable" assumption that a therapist-client relationship has been established in which the professional will provide some level of assistance. Because the nature of this relationship is defined in very broad terms and does not depend on a highly formalized process, it is often one of the easiest elements of a malpractice claim to prove.

In most cases, health care providers have a degree of expertise and knowledge that attracts those in need of services. The very nature of their professional role puts providers in a position of giving care if requested to do so. This is not to say, however, that ambiguous situations cannot arise; in fact, they do all the time. For example, when a therapist is asked for advice by a neighbor whose wife is suicidal. Or when a student asks a psychology teacher who has a part-time private clinical practice if he can talk to him about his suicidal thoughts. Simon (1988) suggests some other instances that may create a doctor-patient relationship, such as: offering a psychological interpretation; writing a prescription; lengthy phone conversations with a prospective client; giving a patient an appointment; telling walk-ins that they will be seen; acting as a substitute therapist; providing treatment during an evaluation; and even providing sample medications.

Lest practitioners become apprehensive about the potential legal consequences of having casual conversations with friends or acquaintances, I should add that it is unlikely that purely social exchanges about mental health matters will be construed as creating a "duty of care." In any situation in which a person appears to think that a practitioner has undertaken a responsibility to provide him with assistance, it is best for the practitioner to take immediate steps to clarify the nature of the relationship to the person. It may also be advisable to refer him to another professional. Taking this extra step will typically relieve you from future liability. In any questionable circumstance, take every reasonable step to clarify the nature and extent of the relationship, and do not take any actions that would create the appearance of a thera- pist-client relationship when it really does not exist.

Nontraditional treatment approaches have introduced ques- tions about the duty and liability of nurses, drug counselors, peer counselors and those who lead support groups, survivor groups or stress seminars. Should these persons be held to the same standards of responsibility as psychologists or psychiatrists? What liability is incurred, for instance, if group members attempt or commit suicide, allegedly prompted by comments, confrontations or actions that took place in their group? It is easy to understand how people who offer specialized counseling services can end up in potentially problematic situations regarding liability. Given the growing tendency of people to sue first and ask questions later, the threat of becoming involved in a lawsuit is not likely to diminish for professionals from a variety of backgrounds and disciplines.

Establishing Standards of Care

The second element a plaintiff must prove in a malpractice lawsuit is that the practitioner's performance did not meet a specific standard of care. Generally speaking, meeting the standard of care means that the practitioner is expected to have and use the knowledge, care and skill ordinarily possessed by other members of his profession who are in good standing. It also requires that the practitioner apply that knowledge using reasonable caution, diligence and sound judgment.

In most malpractice cases, the practitioner's standard of care is evaluated using criteria provided by expert witnesses, but guidance may also be provided by other methods such as state and federal statutes, regulations or practice standards that are formulated by professional organizations. Because these standards are specifically designed to prevent clinical practices that could result in harm or abuse to clients, they are often viewed by the court as establishing the minimum level of care that must be provided to the client. Consequently, any violation of these standards is often viewed by the court as negligence.

Respectable Minority Standard

Because there are a number of recognized schools of thought
and methods of treatment to which practitioners may adhere,
the courts have allowed a practitioner's standard of care to be
judged according to the customary practices of his particular
theoretical school. Known as the "respectable minority standard," this broad legal concept applies to most clinical practices provided that the theoretical perspective is recognized
as an accepted school of thought by a reasonable minority of
the profession. Generally speaking, the concept allows practitioners who use, for example, a classical psychoanalytic perspective to be challenged about the way in which they interpreted the information they obtained, but they may not be
challenged about the theoretical framework they employ,
because it is a recognized psychological paradigm.

Specialists

Practitioners who claim to be specialists in a particular area
will be held to a higher standard of care concerning the application of that specialty than a similarly trained professional
without specialized knowledge or training. For instance, a
therapist who claims to have advanced training in child therapy will be expected to perform at a higher level with regard
to a client who is a child, be more aware of problems specific to this specialty and assume more responsibility for problems that may arise than a therapist without that training.

Expert Witnesses

Clearly, the two points that are the most debatable and most
difficult to establish in a malpractice lawsuit are showing that
a practitioner's conduct was below standard and that the conduct
actually caused the harm to the client. Because neither of

these issues has an accepted objective standard from which courts may seek guidance, they typically call on expert witnesses. It is the function of the expert witness to establish for the court what the appropriate community standard of care should be and to render an opinion as to whether the plaintiff has met that standard. In addition, the expert is often asked to provide an opinion as to causality or foreseeability of the suicide.

A major problem with expert witnesses is that there are no established standards for determining their qualifications. The decision is left solely to the judge who determines whether the witness will be given expert status in his court. He usually bases his decision on the witness' experience, training or reputation. Any witness can be qualified as an expert if he can present convincing evidence that he possesses a sufficient level of expertise in the matter at hand. The more often a witness appears in court as an expert, the greater the likelihood he will receive expert status in subsequent cases.

One of the greatest criticisms about expert testimony is its subjectivity and its reliance on the prior experience and personal judgment of the expert. Because legitimate differences of opinion exist between various schools of thought, there is often no objective way to determine the practical merits of one position over another. In addition, one practitioner's interpretation of the term "reasonable and prudent" may be quite different from another's.

Perhaps the most problematic issue surrounding the topic of expert witnesses is that of ethics. It is a well-known but unfortunate fact that among expert witnesses there are "hired guns" who will make unequivocal statements about clearly equivocal issues pertaining to a practitioner's performance.

When this occurs, even the most accepted clinical practice may appear questionable. For all of these reasons, but especially the last, the issue of what constitutes ethical practice and reasonable scientific judgment in providing expert testimony is a matter of serious, ongoing debate. It is the very real possibility of opposing an expert witness whose opinions are unrealistically rigid or perfectionistic that raises the greatest amount of discussion and concern among professionals facing malpractice claims.

Understandably, practitioners feel particularly vulnerable to the testimony of an expert witness because the opinion of that witness is most likely the standard against which their performance will be judged. Of course, other witnesses with differing opinions can also be qualified as experts, and in these cases, the courtroom can become a forum for a myriad of professional, academic or personal debates that may or may not clarify the questions raised about the practitioner's competence.

When left with a bewildering array of competing and sometimes contradictory views, the judge or jury is placed in a position of reaching decisions based on intangible, subjective opinions rather than objective facts. This means that expert testimony is often judged on style and presentation instead of content. Given the distinct possibility of such complications, it is of the utmost importance that practitioners practice careful risk management by conducting suicide assessments that are above reproach. Unfortunately, expert testimony simply has to be accepted as a challenging aspect of a trial process fraught with unpredictable problems. As such it will always present a potential minefield through which the clinician must walk when confronted with a malpractice suit. Hopefully, sound clinical practice and realistic judgment should provide a trail that will make the journey safer.

Unethical Practices

To establish negligence based on the violation of ethical standards, the unethical practice must be related to the practitioner's failure to exercise the same degree of care and skill that is ordinarily provided by other members of the profession. It is important not to confuse ethical violations with negligence or malpractice. While a breach of ethical standards may be a factor that is considered in determining negligent practice, violations of ethical standards do not, in and of themselves, imply negligence. For example, making derogatory, vulgar or flippant remarks to a client during a counseling session may be viewed as unethical or unprofessional, but it may not be viewed as negligent unless the remarks interfered with the counselor's ability to provide adequate care. Although the client might not have appreciated the tone of the remarks, they may have been therapeutically useful to the client and valuable to the ultimate course of his treatment. While unethical conduct should be discouraged, this example illustrates that it does not, by itself, reduce the quality of care that is provided and it does not, by itself, constitute negligence.

Errors in Judgment

Errors in judgment do not necessarily imply negligence. Courts do not expect practitioners to be perfect when they provide clinical services but to perform them in a reasonable and prudent manner in accordance with accepted principles and the customary practices of their profession. Because there can be legitimate differences of opinion between competent professionals about a particular treatment strategy, and because even under the best circumstances a practitioner can make a mistake, errors in judgment by themselves rarely produce a finding of negligence.

Errors in judgment are typically problematic only if they reflect an imprudent or uncustomary decision-making practice. In other words, if a practitioner decides to provide a service that departs from customary practice and that service is deemed to be inadequate, he may be found negligent. On the other hand, if the practitioner provides an acceptable level of care, but in doing so makes assessment or treatment decisions that ultimately prove to be wrong, he is far less likely to be found negligent.

Clinicians often think that they will be held liable or found negligent if their client kills himself after they diagnosed him as nonsuicidal. For that reason, they often focus all their efforts on ensuring that the client does not commit suicide, sometimes at the expense of engaging in a logical decision-making process. For example, a practitioner assessing a client who has just engaged in a minimally lethal self-destructive act may have ample evidence to conclude that the client was not suicidal, but instead was being manipulative. Nevertheless, because he wants to be absolutely certain that the client will not go on to kill himself, even by accident, he may admit the client to a hospital and place him on suicide precautions with very little data to support the admission. Despite the lack of rational decision-making or the effects of the questionable admission on the client, from the practitioner's perspective, he has taken the necessary steps to guarantee that the client will not kill himself and that he cannot be held liable. However, even in this instance, the practitioner could be sued for harm resulting from involuntary hospitalization and without an adequate rationale for the hospitalization, he could still face an uphill battle in court. This is an example of the way in which clinicians worry about the wrong things while ignoring the right ones because they do not understand the legal issues. From a purely legal perspective, practitioners must understand that it is the *process* that they use to arrive at the decision, not the *outcome*, that is the crucial element in determining negligence or malpractice. This point is so important that it bears repeating. *It is the process, not the outcome, that is critical in evaluating the adequacy of an assessment.*

Legally, clinicians are not expected to be perfect in their assessment of a client's suicidal risk. They are, however, expected to conduct assessments by using all relevant information in a reasonable and prudent manner that reflects a rational decision-making process. While every effort should be made to safeguard a client's life, the critical issue in a lawsuit is not the death itself, but the process the clinician used to make his decisions about managing the case. Consequently, to protect oneself from liability, it is imperative to use an evaluation process that is logical, rational and based at least in large part on objective information. These may not be issues that clinicians pay close attention to while they are conducting an assessment, but they are just the issues that will cause the greatest difficulties in court. And, of course, engaging in a rational decision-making process is not just important for legal purposes, it will also result in a more accurate clinical assessment.

Establishing Harm

The third element that must be proved in a malpractice suit is that the alleged breach of the standard of care caused actual harm to a client. The harm may include physical, psychological or economic consequences that resulted from the negligent behavior of the practitioner. Specific statutes vary from state to state, but generally two types of damage claims may arise. In suicide cases, representatives of the client's estate may bring an action directly on behalf of the client. Actions may also be brought by third parties who suffered physical or emotional injury as a result of a suicide. For example, in one case, the wife of a police officer who committed suicide while under the care of his agency's psychological services department was awarded over $1,000,000 in a malpractice suit. To receive financial compensation in third-party actions, plaintiffs must demonstrate that they have suffered a specific and identifiable harm, either of a physical or psychological nature, or both. The actual dollar amounts of compensation vary greatly, depending on the jury's subjective assessment of the damage.

When there has been a completed or attempted suicide that resulted in a physical injury or disability, obviously it is not hard to show that harm was caused. For this reason, in suicide cases, the question of harm is often an uncontested or minimally contested element of the suit. However, in cases where people try to claim that they also suffered harm as a result of a suicide, the extent of the harm and the concomitant compensation are often an issue because there may be considerable disagreement about the relationship between the victim and the plaintiffs. There is also ample opportunity for debate about the potential financial value to be affixed to the harm, that is, if it was found to exist in the first place.

Establishing Causation of Harm

The fourth element that must be proved by the plaintiff in a malpractice suit is the proximate or direct causation of the harm. To prove proximate cause, the harm that is being claimed must be directly caused by the negligent behavior of the practitioner. This element — highly debated and often debatable — is usually the most difficult element to prove in a lawsuit because there are so many factors other than the actions of the practitioner that could have contributed, either directly or indirectly, to the suicidal behavior of the client.

The actions of the client himself, for example, may be shown to contribute to the harm that was inflicted. Clients with psychiatric conditions often contribute to their own harm because of the psychological dynamics of their mental illness. This is clearly not the clinician's fault. Clients may be so influenced by various internal, idiosyncratic, psychological factors that their behavior is difficult if not impossible to predict, despite how much the clinician knows about them. Also, some clients may withhold vital information about themselves that, had the clinician known, might have changed his assessment of risk. In addition, there may be environmental, social and personal variables in the client's life, beyond the clinician's control, that make it nearly impossible to place sole responsibility for the suicide on the clinician. Thus, in most cases, determining that the behavior of the clinician was the sole cause of the suicide is difficult to establish. Nevertheless, the plaintiff must demonstrate that the clinician's negligence was the direct cause of the harm, and moreover, that without the negligent behavior, the harm would not have occurred.

Foreseeability

Over the years, courts have expanded the definition of proximate cause to include the concept of foreseeability. By applying this principle, plaintiffs need not demonstrate a direct link between a practitioner's actions and the death. Rather, they only must show that the practitioner should have been able to foresee the behavior. In other words, the concept of foreseeability asserts that the practitioner had or should have been aware of information, such as established risk factors, that would have alerted him in advance that the client was at high risk for harm. Expanding the concept of proximate cause to include foreseeability assumes that a reasonable and prudent clinician would have been able to predict the harmful behavior, given the same information, or that he should have obtained other, more relevant information that would have made the suicide predictable.

While adding the concept of foreseeability does provide somewhat more latitude to support the plaintiff's allegations, it is not any easier to establish and it poses no greater risk to the competent, well-informed practitioner. In evaluating either proximate cause or foreseeability, without the nexus or linkage between the practitioner's behavior and the harm, negligence cannot be established, regardless of the weight of any other element.

LESSONS FROM THE LEGAL ARENA

It should be remembered that the number of cases won against health care professionals each year is still fairly small and while the number of malpractice suits is clearly on the rise, the threat of a lawsuit should not become the source of unrealistic fear for practitioners. Clinicians whose assessments are not thorough and well documented are the ones who find themselves in an uphill struggle when it comes time to defend their actions in court. On the other hand, clinicians who know the questions and issues that could arise if they are sued, and who therefore conduct assessments that address these issues, will reduce their chances of being found liable.

It is a mistake for mental health professionals to view the legal system as their enemy. Due to the lack of effective guidelines and treatment standards, it is understandable that the courts have become the final arbitrator in determining the adequacy of professional care. The courts are concerned with being fair in their evaluation of the facts and opinions provided. Because they realize that practitioners are not perfect, courts do not judge them against perfection, but against a reasonable and prudent standard of performance.

Despite this, the legal arena is fraught with potential problems. Furthermore, it is an arena that is foreign to most mental health professionals. Therefore, it behooves clinicians to become familiar with the legal criteria that will be used to judge their performance and to measure the quality of their assessments against these criteria. To be safe, mental health professionals must not only ask themselves "Is my assessment good enough?" but also "How will my actions be judged in court if my client commits suicide?" The issue that the court will determine is not whether the clinician was right, but whether his actions were consistent with a reasonable and accepted standard of care. Remember also that all of the decisions you made in the case must be considered suitable and defensible by an impartial third party.

Taking the time to perform an assessment with a reasonable degree of care and skill is worthwhile, particularly considering the possible consequences of not doing so. A careful assessment will allow for a more thorough, rational and relevant treatment process that will benefit the client and at the same time protect the professional from legal vulnerability. The primary goal of the H.E.L.P.E.R. suicide assessment system is to show practitioners how to conduct comprehensive assessments that will not only increase their chances of accurately assessing risk in their clients but will also serve to protect them should they ever be sued.

References

Barraclough, B.M., Bunch, J., Nelson, B. and Sainsbury, P. (1974). A hundred cases of suicide. *British Journal of Psychiatry* 125:355-373.

Beck, A.T., Resnik, H.L.P. and Lettieri, D.J. (eds.) (1986). *The Prediction of Suicide*. Philadelphia: The Charles Press, Publishers.

Beck, A.T., Steer, R. and Trexler, L.D. (1989). Alcohol abuse and eventual suicide. *Journal of Studies on Alcohol* 50:202-209.

Bellamy, W.A. (1962). Malpractice risks confronting the psychiatrist: a nationwide fifteen-year study of appellate court cases, 1946-1961. *American Journal of Psychiatry* 118:769-780.

Berman, A. (1986). A critical look at our adolescence: notes on turning 18 (and 75). *Suicide and Life-Threatening Behavior* 16(1):1-12.

Berman, A.L. and Jobes, D.A. (1991). *Adolescent Suicide: Assessment and Intervention*. Washington, D.C.: American Psychological Association.

Black, D.W. and Winokur, G. (1988). Age, mortality and chronic schizophrenia. *Schizophrenia Research* 1:267-272.

Blatt, S.J. (1995). The destructiveness of perfectionism: implications for the treatment of depression. *American Psychologist* 50(12):1003-1020.

Bongar, B. (1991). *The Suicidal Patient: Clinical and Legal Standards of Care*. Washington, DC: American Psychological Association.

Bongar, B. (1993). Consultation and the suicidal patient. *Suicide and Life-Threatening Behavior* 23(4):299-306.

Bongar, B. and Harmatz, M. (1989). Graduate training in clinical psychology and the study of suicide. *Professional Psychology: Research and Practice* 20(4):209-213.

Bongar, B., Maris, R.W., Berman, A.L. and Litman, R.E. (1992). Outpatient standards of care and the suicidal patient. *Suicide and Life-Threatening Behavior* 22(4):453-478.

Bongar, B., Maris, R.W., Berman, A.L. and Litman, R.E. (1993). Inpatient standards of care and the suicidal patient: general clinical formulations and legal considerations. *Suicide and Life-Threatening Behavior* 23(3):245-256.

Brent, D.A., Kupfer, D.J., Bromet, E.J. and Dew, M.A. (1988). The assessment and treatment of patients at risk for suicide. In A.J. Frances and R.E. Hales (eds.), *American Psychiatric Press Review of Psychiatry,* Vol. 7. Washington, DC: American Psychiatric Press.

Brent, D.A., Perper, J.A., and Allman, C.J., et al. (1991). The presence and accessibility of firearms in the homes of adolescent suicides: a case-control study. *Journal of the American Medical Association* 266:2989-2995.

Brown, H.N. (1987). The impact of suicides on therapists in training. *Comprehensive Psychiatry* 28(2):101-112.

Canetto, S.S. (1992-93). She died for love and he for glory. *Omega* 26:1-17.

Chemtob, C.M., Bauer, G.B., Hamada, R.S., et al. (1989). Patient suicide: occupational hazard for psychologists and psychiatrists. *Professional Psychology: Research and Practice* 20(5):294-300.

Chemtob, C.M., Hamada, R.S., Bauer, G.B., et al. (1988). Patient suicide: frequency and impact on psychiatrists. *American Journal of Psychiatry* 145:224-228.

Clark, D.C. and Fawcett, J.A. (1992). Review of empirical risk factors for evaluation of the suicidal patient. In B. Bonger (ed.), *Suicide: Guidelines for Assessment, Management and Treatment*. New York: Oxford University Press.

Cohen, S., Leonard, C.V. and Farberow, N.L. (1964). Tranquilizers and suicide in the schizophrenic patient. *Archives of General Psychiatry* 11:312-321.

Cornwell, Y. (1994). Suicide and terminal illness: lessons from the HIV pandemic. *Crisis* 15:2.

DiClemente, R.J., Ponton, L.E. and Hartley, D. (1991). Prevalence and correlates of cutting behavior: risk for HIV transmission. *Journal of the American Academy of Child and Adolescent Psychiatry* 30:735-739.

Dooley, D., Catalano, R., Rook, K. and Serxner, S. (1989). Economic stress and suicide. *Suicide and Life-Threatening Behavior* 19:337-351.

Dorpat, T.L. and Ripley, H.S. (1960). A study of suicide in the Seattle area. *Comprehensive Psychiatry* 1.

Drake, R.E., Gates, C., Whitaker, A. and Cotton, P. (1985). Suicide among schizophrenics. *Comprehensive Psychiatry* 26:90-100.

Dublin, L. (1963). *Suicide*. New York: Ronald Press.

Egeland, J. and Sussex, J. (1985). Suicide and family loading for affective disorders. *Journal of the American Medical Association* 254:915-918.

Ellis, A. (1962). *Reason and Emotion in Psychotherapy*. New York: Lyle Stuart.

Ellis, T.E. and Ratliff, K.G. (1986). Cognitive characteristics of suicidal and nonsuicidal psychiatric patients. *Cognitive Therapy and Research* 10:625-634.

Farber, M.L. (1968). *Theory of Suicide*. New York: Funk & Wagnalls.

Farberow, N.L. and Shneidman, E.S. (eds.) (1961). *The Cry for Help*. New York: McGraw-Hill.

Fawcett, J.A. (1988). Predictors of early suicide identification and appropriate intervention. *Journal of Clinical Psychiatry* 49 (suppl. 10):7-8.

Festinger, L. (1957). *A Theory of Cognitive Dissonance.* Evanston, IL: Row, Peterson.

Fleming, J.E., Boyle, M. and Offord, D.R: (1993). The outcome of adolescent depression in the Ontario child health study follow-up. *Journal of the American Academy of Child and Adolescent Psychiatry* 32(1):28.

Frances, R.J., Franklin, J. and Flavin, D.K. (1987). Suicide and alcoholism. *American Journal of Drug and Alcohol Abuse* 13:327-341.

Fremouw, W.J., de Perczel, M. and Ellis, T.E. (1990). *Suicide Risk: Assessment and Response Guidelines.* New York: Pergamon Press.

Ganzler, S. (1967). Some interpersonal and social dimensions of suicidal behavior. *Dissertation Abstracts* 28B:1192-1193.

Garland, A.F. and Zigler, E. (1993). Adolescent suicide prevention: current research and social policy implications. *American Psychologist* 48(2):169-182.

Garrison, C.Z. (1992). Demographic predictors of suicide. In R.W. Maris, A.L. Berman, J.T. Maltsberger and R.I.Yufit (eds.), *Assessment and Prediction of Suicide.* New York: The Guilford Press.

Goldman, S. and Beardslee, W.R. (1999). Suicide in children and adolescents. In D.G. Jacobs (ed.), *The Harvard Medical School Guide to Suicide Assessment and Intervention.* San Francisco: Jossey-Bass.

Goodwin, F.K. and Jamison, K.R. (1990). *Manic-Depressive Illness.* New York: Oxford University Press.

Gutheil, T.G. (1980). Paranoia and progress notes: a guide to forensically informed psychiatric record-keeping. *Hospital and Community Psychiatry* 31(7):479-482.

Heikkinen, M., Hillevi, A. and Lonnqvist, J. (1993) Life events and social support in suicide. *Suicide and Life-*

Threatening Behavior 23(4):343-358.

Henn, R.F. (1978). Patient suicide as part of psychiatric residency. *American Journal of Psychiatry* 135 (6):745-746.

Henriksson, M.M., Aro, H.M., Marttunen, M.J., Heikkinen, M.E., Isomatesa, E.T., Kuoppasalmi, K.I. and Lonnqvist, J. (1993). Mental disorders and comorbidity in suicide. *American Journal of Psychiatry* 150(6):935-940.

Hirschfeld, R.M.A. and Davidson, L. (1988). Clinical risk factors for suicide. *Psychiatric Annual* 18:628-635.

Hoberman, H.M. and Garfindel, B.D. (1988) Completed suicide in children and adolescents. *Journal of the American Academy of Child and Adolescent Psychiatry* 27:689-695.

Hornig, C.D. and McNally, R.J. (1995). Panic disorder and suicide attempt: a reanalysis of data from the Epidemiologic Catchment Area Study. *British Journal of Psychiatry* 167:76-79.

Jones, I.H., Congiu, L., Stevenson, J., Strauss, N. and Frei, D.Z. (1979). A biological approach to two forms of human self-injury. *Journal of Nervous and Mental Disease* 167:74-78.

Jones, J.S., Stein, D.J. and Stanley, B. (1994). Negative and depressive symptoms in suicidal schizophrenia. *Acta Psychiatrica Scandinavica* 89:81-87.

Kizer, K.W., Green, M., Perkins, C.I., Doebbert, G. and Hughes, M.J. (1988). AIDS and suicide in California. *Journal of American Medical Association* 260(13):881.

Kleck, G. (1988). Miscounting suicides. *Suicide and Life-Threatening Behavior* 18:219-236.

Lester, D. (1986). Genetics, twin studies and suicide. *Suicide and Life-Threatening Behavior* 16:274-285.

Lester, D. (1987). *Suicide as a Learned Behavior*. Springfield, IL: Charles C Thomas.

Lester, D. (1989). *Questions and Answers about Suicide*. Philadelphia: The Charles Press, Publishers.

Lester, D. (1992a). Alcoholism and drug abuse. In R.W. Maris,

A.L. Berman, J.T. Maltsberger and R.I. Yufit (eds.), *Assessment and Prediction of Suicide*. New York: The Guilford Press.

Lester, D. (1992b). *Why People Kill Themselves: A 1990's Summary of Research Findings on Suicidal Behavior*. Springfield, IL: Charles C Thomas.

Lester, D. (1997). *Making Sense of Suicide*. Philadelphia: The Charles Press, Publishers.

Lester, D. and Danto, B.L. (1993). *Suicide Behind Bars: Prediction and Prevention*. Philadelphia: The Charles Press, Publishers.

Lester, D. and Tallmer, M. (1994). *Now I Lay Me Down: Suicide in the Elderly*. Philadelphia: The Charles Press, Publishers.

Lester, D., Beck, A.T. and Trexler, L. (1975). Extrapolation from attempted suicides to completed suicides. *Journal of Abnormal Psychology* 84:563-566.

Lester, D., Beck, A.T. and Trexler, L. (1979). Extrapolation from attempted suicides to completed suicides: a follow-up. *Journal of Abnormal Psychology* 88:78-80.

Linehan, M.M., Goodstein, J.L., Nielsen, S.L. and Chiles, J.A. (1983). Reasons for staying alive when you're thinking of killing yourself. *Journal of Consulting and Clinical Psychology* 51:276-286.

Lonnqvist, J. and Ostramo, A. (1987). Suicide mortality after the first suicide attempt. In R. Yufit (ed.), *Proceedings of the 20th Annual Conference*. Denver: American Association of Suicidology.

Lyons, M. (1985). Observable and subjective factors associated with attempted suicide in later life. *Suicide and Life-Threatening Behavior* 15:168-183.

Maltsberger, J.T. (1988). Suicide danger: clinical estimation and decision. *Suicide and Life-Threatening Behavior* 18(1):47-54.

Maris, R.W. (1981). *Pathways to Suicide: A Survey of Self-*

Destructive Behaviors. Baltimore: Johns Hopkins University Press.

Maris, R.W. (1992). The relationship of nonfatal suicide attempts to completed suicides. In R.W. Maris, A.L. Berman, J.T. Maltsberger and R.I. Yufit (eds.), *Assessment and Prediction of Suicide*. New York: The Guilford Press.

Maris, R.W., Berman, A.L., Maltsberger, J.T. and Yufit, R.I. (eds.) (1992). *Assessment and Prediction of Suicide*. New York: The Guilford Press.

Martinez, M.E. (1980). Manipulative self-injurious behavior in correctional settings. *Journal of Offender Counseling Services and Rehabilitation* 4:275-283.

Marzuk, P.M., Tierney, H., Tardiff, K., Gross, E.M., Morgan, E.B., Shu, M.A. and Mann, J.J. (1988). Increased risk of suicide in persons with AIDS. *Journal of the American Medical Association* 259(9):1333-1337.

Maultsby, M.C. (1975). *Help Yourself to Happiness Through Rational Self-Counseling*. New York: Institute for Rational Living.

Mayo, D.J. (1992). What is being predicted? The definition of "suicide." In R.W. Maris, A.L. Berman, J.T. Maltsberger and R.I. Yufit (eds.), *Assessment and Prediction of Suicide*. New York: The Guilford Press.

McIntosh, J. L. (1992). Methods of suicide. In R.W. Maris, A.L. Berman, J.T. Maltsberger and R.I. Yufit (eds.), *Assessment and Prediction of Suicide*. New York: The Guilford Press.

McMahon, B. and Pugh, T. (1965). Suicide in the widowed. *American Journal of Epidemiology* 81:23-31.

Meloy, J.R. (1994). Assessment of Violence Potential. Workshop sponsored by Specialized Training Services, Inc., Minneapolis.

Miles, C.P. (1977). Conditions predisposing to suicide: a review. *Journal of Nervous and Mental Diseases* 164:231-247.

Miller, D.H. Suicidal careers. *Dissertation Abstracts* 28A:

4720, 1968.

Miller, M. (1979). *Suicide After Sixty.* New York: Springer.

Monahan, J. and Steadman, H.J. (1996). Violent storms and violent people: how meteorology can inform risk communications in mental health law. *American Psychologist* 51:931-938.

Moscicki, E.K., O'Carroll, P. and Lock, B.Z. (1989). Suicidal Ideation and Attempts. In U.S. Department of Health and Human Services, *Report of the Secretary's Task Force on Youth Suicide*, Vol. 4. Washington, DC: U.S. Government Printing Office.

Motto, J.A. (1999). Critical points in the assessment and management of suicide risk. In J.G. Jacobs (ed.), *The Harvard Medical School Guide to Suicide Assessment and Intervention*. San Francisco: Jossey-Bass.

Murphy, G.E. and Robins, E. (1967). Social factors in suicide. *Journal of the American Medical Association* 199:303-308.

Murphy, G.E., Wetzel, R.D., Robins, E. and McEvoy, L. (1992). Multiple risk factors predict suicide in alcoholism. *Archives of General Psychiatry* 49:459-463.

National Center for Health Statistics (1997). Report of final mortality statistics, 1995. *Monthly Vital Statistics Report* 45(11): Supp.2.

Pallis, D. and Barraclough, M.M. (1977-78). Seriousness of suicide attempt and future risk of suicide. *Omega* 8:141-149.

Patsiokas, A.T., Clum, G.A. and Luscomb, R.L. (1979). Cognitive characteristics of suicide attempters. *Journal of Consulting and Clinical Psychology* 47:478-484.

Pattison, E.M. and Kahan, J. (1983). The deliberate self-harm syndrome. *American Journal of Psychiatry* 140:867-872.

Phillips, D.P. and Ruth, T.E. (1993). Adequacy of official suicide statistics for scientific research and public policy. *Suicide and Life-Threatening Behavior* 23(4):307.

Pierce, D. (1981). The predictive validation of a suicide intent scale. *British Journal of Psychiatry* 139:391-396.

Pierce, D. (1984). Suicidal intent and repeated self-harm. *Psychological Medicine* 14:655-659.

Plutchik, R., van Praag, H.M. and Conte, H.R. (1989). Correlates of suicide and violence risk. III. A two-stage model of countervailing forces. *Psychiatric Research* 28:215-225.

Pokorny, A.D. (1983). Prediction of suicide in psychiatric patients. *Archives of General Psychiatry* 40:249-257.

Power, K.G. and Spencer, A.P. (1987). Parasuicidal behavior in detained Scottish young offenders. *International Journal of Offender Therapy* 31:227-235.

Price, J.H., Everett, S.A., Bedell, A.W. and Telljohann, S.K. (1997). Reduction of firearm-related violence through firearm safety counseling: the role of family physicians. *Archives of Family Medicine* 6:79-83.

Rachlin, S. (1984). Double jeopardy: suicide and malpractice. *General Hospital Psychiatry* 6:302-307.

Renolds, P. and Eaton, P. (1986). Multiple attempters of suicide presenting at an emergency department. *Canadian Journal of Psychiatry* 31:328-330.

Resnick, P. (1994). Clinical Assessment of Malingering and Deception. Workshop sponsored by Specialized Training Services, Inc., Chicago.

Rich, C.L. and Runeson, B.S. (1992). Similarities in diagnostic comorbidity between suicide among young people in Sweden and the United States. *Acta Psychiatrica Scandinavica* 86:335-339.

Rich, C.L., Young, D. and Fowler, R.C. (1986). San Diego Suicide Study: I. Young vs. old subjects. *Archives of General Psychiatry* 43:577-582.

Richman, J. and Eyman, J. (1990). Psychotherapy of suicide. In D. Lester (ed.), *Current Concepts of Suicide*. Philadelphia: The Charles Press, Publishers.

Robertson, J.D. (1988). *Psychiatric Malpractice: Liability of*

Mental Health Professionals. New York: John Wiley and Sons.

Robins, E., Gassner, S., Kayes, J., Wilkinson, R.H. and Murphy, G.E. (1959). The communication of suicidal intent: a study of 134 consecutive cases of successful suicide. *American Journal of Psychiatry* 115:724-733.

Robins, E., Murphy, G.E., Wilkinson, R.H., Gassner, S. and Kayes, J. (1959). Some clinical considerations in the prevention of suicide based on a study of 134 successful suicides. *American Journal of Public Health* 49:888-899.

Roy, A. (1982). Suicide in chronic schizophrenia. *British Journal of Psychiatry* 141:171-177.

Roy, A. (1986). Depression, attempted suicide and suicide in patients with chronic schizophrenia. *Psychiatric Clinics of North America* 9(1):193-206.

Roy, A. and Linnoila, M. (1986). Alcoholism and suicide. *Suicide and Life-Threatening Behavior* 16:244-276.

Roy, A., Segal, N., Centerwall, B. and Robinette, D. (1990). Suicide in twins. *Archives of General Psychiatry* 48:29-32.

Salloum, I.M., Daley, D.C. and Cornelius, J.R. (1996). Disproportionate lethality in psychiatric patients with concurrent alcohol and cocaine abuse. *American Journal of Psychiatry* 153:953-955.

Schotte, D.E. and Clum, G.A. (1987). Problem-solving skills in suicidal psychiatric patients. *Journal of Consulting and Clinical Psychology* 55:49-54.

Schulsinger, F., Ketty, S.S., Rosenthal, D. and Wender, P.H. (1979). A family study of suicide. In M. Schou and E. Stromgren (eds.), *Origin, Prevention and Treatment of Affective Disorders*. New York: Academic Press.

Shafii, M., Carrigan, S., Whittinghill, J.R. and Derrick, A. (1985). Psychological autopsy of completed suicide in children and adolescents. *American Journal of Psychiatry* 142:1061-1064.

Shneidman, E.S. (1985). *Definition of Suicide*. New York: John Wiley and Sons.

Sifneos, P. (1966). Manipulative suicide. *Psychiatric Quarterly* 40:525-537.

Simon, R.I. (1988). *Concise Guide to Clinical Psychiatry and the Law*. Washington, DC: American Psychiatric Press.

Simon, R.I. (1992). *Clinical Psychiatry and the Law*, 2nd ed. Washington, DC: American Psychiatric Press.

Smith, K. and Crawford, S. (1986). Suicidal behavior among normal high school students. *Suicide and Life-Threatening Behavior* 16:313-325.

Smith, K. and Eyman, J. (1988). Ego structure and object differentiation in suicidal patients. In H.D. Lerner and P.M Lerner (eds.), *Primitive Mental States and the Rorschach*. Madison, CT: International Universities Press.

Soloff, P.H., Lis, J.A. and Kelly, T. (1994). Risk factors for suicidal behavior in borderline personality disorder. *American Journal of Psychiatry* 151:1316-1323.

Spirito, A., Williams, C.A., Stark, L.J. and Hart, K.J. (1988). The hopelessness scale for children: psychometric properties with normal and emotionally disturbed adolescents. *Journal of Abnormal Child Psychology* 16:445-458.

Stack, S. (1992). Marriage, family, religion and suicide. In R.W. Maris, A.L. Berman, J.T. Maltsberger and R.I.Yufit (eds.), *Assessment and Prediction of Suicide*. New York: The Guilford Press.

Stelmachers, Z.T. and Sherman, R.E. (1989). The case vignette method of suicide assessment. In R.W. Maris, et al. (eds.), *Assessment and Prediction of Suicide*. New York: The Guilford Press.

Stillion, J.M., McDowell, E.E. and May, J.H. (1989). *Suicide Across the Lifespan*. Washington, DC: Hemisphere.

Strasburger, L.H. and Welpton, S.S. (1991). Elderly suicide: minimizing risk for patient and professional. *Journal of Geriatric Psychiatry* 24(2):235-259.

Stromberg, C.D. (1988). *The Psychologist's Legal Handbook*. Washington, DC: The Council for the National Register of

Health Service Providers in Psychology.

Suokas, J. and Lonnqvist, J.K. (1995). Suicide attempts in which alcohol is involved: a special group in general hospital emergency rooms. *Acta Psychiatrica Scandinavica* 91:36-40.

Tanney, B.L. (1992). Mental disorders, psychiatric patients and suicide. In R.W. Maris, A.L. Berman, J.T. Maltsberger and R.I. Yufit (eds.), *Assessment and Prediction of Suicide*. New York: The Guilford Press.

Tejedor, M.C., Castillon, J., Percay, J., Puigdellivol, M. and Turnes, E. (1987). Suicidal behavior in schizophrenics. *Crisis* 8:151-161.

Topol, P. and Reznikoff, M. (1982). Perceived peer and family relationships, hopelessness and loss of control as factors in adolescent suicide attempts. *Suicide and Life-Threatening Behavior* 12:141-150.

Tsuang, M.T., Fleming, J.A. and Simpson, J.C. (1999). Suicide and schizophrenia. In D.G. Jacobs (ed.), *The Harvard Medical School Guide to Suicide Assessment and Intervention*. San Francisco: Jossey-Bass.

Walsh, B.W. and Rosen, P.M. (1988). *Self-Mutilation*. New York: The Guilford Press.

Wanstall, K. and Oei, T.P. (1989). Delicate wrist-cutting behavior in adult psychiatric patients: a review. *Australian Psychologist* 24(1):13-25.

Weishaar, M.E. and Beck, A.T. (1992). Clinical and cognitive predictors of suicide. In R.W. Maris, A.L. Berman, J.T. Maltsberger and R.I.Yufit (eds.), *Assessment and Prediction of Suicide*. New York: The Guilford Press.

Weissman, M.M., Kleerman, G.L., Markowitz, J.S., et al. (1989). Suicidal ideation and suicide attempts in panic disorder and attacks. *New England Journal of Medicine* 3211:1209-1214.

Welte, J., Able, E. and Wieczorek, W. (1988). The role of alcohol in studies in Erie County, NY, 1972-1984. *Public*

Health Reports 103:648-652.

Wender, P.H., Kety, S.S., Rosenthal, D., Schulsinger, F., Ortmann, J. and Lunde, I. (1986). Psychiatric disorders in the biological and adoptive families of adopted individuals with affective disorders. *Archives of General Psychiatry* 43:923-929.

White, T.W. (1993a). The H.E.L.P.E.R. Suicide Assessment Protocol. Workshop presented at the Third Annual Mental Health in Corrections Symposium, Kansas City, MO.

White, T.W. (1993b). Clinical-Legal Issues Affecting Suicide Prevention. Paper presented at the 26th Annual Conference, American Association of Suicidology, San Francisco.

White, T.W. and Schimmel, D.J. (1993). Suicide prevention: a successful five-step program. In Lindsay M. Hayes (ed.), *Prison Suicide: An Overview and Guide to Prevention*. Washington, DC: National Institute of Corrections, U.S. Department of Justice.

Whitters, A.C., Cedoret, R.J. and Widmer, R.B. (1985). Factors associated with suicide attempts in alcohol abusers. *Journal of Affective Disorders* 9:19-23.

Wolk-Wasserman, D. (1986). Suicidal communications of persons attempting suicide and response of significant others. *Acta Psychiatrica Scandinavica* 73:481-499.

Wrobleski, A. and McIntosh, J.L. (1986). Clues to suicide and suicide survivors. In R. Cohen-Sandler (ed.), *Proceedings of the 19th Annual Meeting*. Denver: American Association of Suicidology.

APPENDIX

Sample Risk Assessment Report: A Low-Risk Example

BASIC INFORMATION

John Smith is a 28-year-old Caucasian male who was seen individually by me, as an emergency referral, in the Greene County Jail, in Waynesburg, Pennsylvania, on June 29, 1999. The interview took place in a private office in the jail complex and lasted for approximately 1 hour. I had never seen Mr. Smith before, but prior to interviewing him, I had an opportunity to review records that were provided to me by correctional personnel.

REASON FOR ASSESSMENT

After threatening to kill himself, Mr. Smith was referred for assessment on the morning of December 18, 1998, by Robert Johnson, a member of the correctional staff at Greene County Jail. Mr. Smith was being held on a drug possession charge and during an interview with probation staff shortly after his arrest, he threatened to kill himself if they did not transfer him to Longview State Hospital where he thought he would get better treatment. Mr. Smith told the probation officer that he had a long history of drug addiction and emotional problems and that he had attempted suicide many times in the past. He said that he needed treatment, not imprisonment, and that if he was not moved immediately, he would kill himself. Jail personnel placed Mr. Smith in secure housing to preclude any suicidal actions and referred him for assessment to determine if he was indeed suicidal and if he required hospitalization to prevent him from killing himself.

SOURCES OF INFORMATION

According to past arrest and criminal records obtained by jail personnel, Mr. Smith has several previous arrests and, since he was 16, he has spent a total of 5 years in custody. His records also indicated that he has had a long history of mental health problems for which he received treatment and that he has attempted suicide many times. The records they provided me address only the most recent portion of his treatment, dating back to August 1995. When I asked Mr. Smith if I could take a look at the records and documentation that had been kept on him by other mental health care providers, he told me that he did not object and he signed the release forms that allowed me to do so.

Mr. Smith's available criminal records only cover the last 3½ years. During that time he was in jail on three occasions and was in state prison for approximately 11 months. The material indicates that there are four documented episodes during that period in which Mr. Smith threatened or attempted suicide. In August 1995, Mr. Smith was taken to jail after causing a disturbance in the county social service office. He refused to leave the building and threatened to kill himself if he was not permitted to remain on public assistance. He was taken to jail and released the following day. Mr. Smith said that he did not intend to kill himself, but felt that he could scare the social worker into giving him extra food stamps. He added that it worked out anyway because he was fed while he was in jail. The next documented incident occurred in

October 1995, when he was again in jail on drug charges. At that time he cut his left wrist. According to reports, this was a relatively superficial injury that required three stitches. Mr. Smith said he cut himself because he was mad at the guards because they would not give him his cigarettes. Following an 11-month prison sentence, Mr. Smith was released from custody on September 14, 1996. No records were immediately available for this period of incarceration, but Mr. Smith said that he got along relatively well during that time. On March 18, 1997, he was placed in jail after police were called to a domestic disturbance between Mr. Smith and his girlfriend. He was highly intoxicated at the time and while in custody broke a window and used the glass to cut his right forearm severely enough to require 13 stitches. Mr. Smith said that he could not remember much about the incident because he had been drinking, but said that he was having trouble with the person who was in the cell with him and that the guards would not move him. He told them that if he wasn't moved, he would kill himself. They didn't pay any attention to his threats, so he cut himself. When questioned, he said that after he was stitched up, he was moved to another cell. The last incident occurred in September 1998, requiring him to be taken to a hospital emergency room for treatment. Mr. Smith said that he had been living with his girlfriend for about 8 months. They would fight often and the police were called on several occasions. He said that during many of their arguments, he had threatened to kill himself because she threatened to leave him. Usually things worked out, but on this particular evening they had both been drinking heavily and she told him she didn't care if he killed himself and to get out of her apartment. Realizing that he had nowhere else to go, his threats escalated until he felt forced to "go through with it" to prove he was "serious." While they were both standing in the kitchen, he grabbed a knife from the sink and impulsively slashed his left wrist. Medical reports indicated that the cut, while deep and long, was not life-threatening. It did, however, cut several large blood vessels and required 25 stitches to close.

PHYSICAL APPEARANCE AND BEHAVIORAL OBSERVATIONS

Mr. Smith was brought to the interview room by correctional staff. He was still wearing his own clothing, which consisted of a t-shirt, blue jeans and tennis shoes. His clothing was inexpensive and well worn. Mr. Smith appeared to be in good physical condition, but he had long, poorly kept hair, several days of beard growth and generally displayed a rather disheveled appearance. While his appearance could probably be attributed in part to the emotional stress of being arrested and held in a jail cell, the fact that he had only been in custody for a few hours at the time I saw him indicated to me that his poor hygiene and careless look were probably typical for him. Mr. Smith's general appearance and clothing indicated that he probably had limited financial means, but regardless of his resources, his grooming suggested that Mr. Smith was an individual who was not overly concerned with the way he looked. One may assume that he had little interest in making a favorable social impression.

When Mr. Smith arrived for the interview and I introduced myself, he sat down across from me without making eye contact or overtly acknowledging my presence. The first statement he made was to ask for a cigarette. When I informed him that smoking was not allowed in this area, he became angry, saying that it was a stupid rule and that he needed a cigarette to help him relax. He then asked me how I could help him get out of there if I couldn't even get him a cigarette. This interchange was fairly typical of Mr. Smith's behavior throughout the interview. Most of the time he tried to control the conversation and responded in an argumentative and confrontational manner when his point of view was questioned. In fact, the most distinguishing feature of Mr. Smith's behavior during the interview was his shifting level of hostility which was punctuated by outbursts of anger following any comment he perceived as conflicting with his views. For the most part, he was engaged and attentive when he was talking, but he seemed to lose interest when I was talking to him. As such, the interview was quite volatile, ranging from relatively calm periods when he was able to control the course of the conversation, to explosive outbursts when things did not go his way.

Throughout the interview Mr. Smith was talkative, but only marginally informative. The historical information he presented was generally consistent with material in his records, but there were gaps and inconsistencies in his accounts. He changed subjects frequently and responded to most of my direct questions in an ambiguous or imprecise manner. He rarely talked about emotional matters, preferring instead to talk about material that highlighted what he viewed as mistreatment by others. His rather suspicious and distrusting attitude about people was a frequent and recurring theme during the interview. In general, he rarely took responsibility for his actions and saw himself as a victim of personal injustices caused by others.

HISTORICAL FACTORS

Personal History

Mr. Smith has been diagnosed with a number of personality disorders and has a long-standing substance abuse problem for which previous treatment has been ineffective. Mr. Smith reported countless contacts with mental health professionals over the years. Given his involvement with the criminal justice system and social service agencies, this is not surprising, particularly with his history of chemical abuse and suicide attempts. Mr. Smith said that off and on during the times when he was not incarcerated, he received individual psychotherapy, group therapy, drug counseling and attended Alcoholics Anonymous meetings. While he was in prison, he also received drug treatment and was involved in many counseling programs. He said that he found most of the counseling to be "a total waste of time" and that he derived the greatest benefit from taking medication for his anxiety.

Mr. Smith said he has made numerous suicide attempts in his lifetime. As proof of this, he eagerly showed me his arms, which had countless scars on both the inner and outer forearms. He said that over the years he has thought about killing himself and threatened to do as many as 50 times. He also said that he had made actual suicide attempts about 20 times. He made his first suicide attempt at the age of 16, he told me, after he had been placed in a juvenile detention center because he stole a car and ran away from his foster parents' home.

Mr. Smith said that he made several suicide attempts while he was in custody and that he tried to kill himself because people would not listen to him or refused to give him something he wanted. A review of his medical records (which date back only to 1995) verifies that Mr. Smith did indeed engage in self-destructive behavior on three occasions: once in 1995, once in 1997 while in custody and once in September of 1998, after an argument with a girlfriend. Each of these reports indicated the act involved cutting his wrists. He reported that he usually cut his wrists using anything that was available. He also said that he has taken pills on two occasions, but this is not verified in the records. When I asked him if he was trying to die when he engaged in these behaviors, he said that he to die when he engaged in these behaviors, he said that he "really wasn't sure." He admitted, however, that in several of the "attempts" that he made while he was in jail, his real goal was to get the attention of the guards. He added that the guards would only take his attempt seriously if "they saw blood." When asked about the severity of his injuries on these occasions, Mr. Smith said that most of the cuts did not require more than a few stitches, but the last two "attempts" were more serious and he had to be taken to the hospital to save his life.

Family History

Mr. Smith stated, "I have no family at all." He said that he was raised in foster care since the age of 8 when he was taken from his natural mother by the Greene County Department of Social Services. He said that she was a "low-down junkie" who was addicted to cocaine and that she couldn't take care of herself, much less him. He has not seen her since he was removed from her care and he told me that "she has never even bothered to find out if I'm still alive." Records obtained from probation officials generally verify Mr. Smith's account of his family history. They indicate that he has been in and out of group homes, detention centers, jails and social service agencies since the age of 8. I could not find proof of any other living relatives and there is no record of his mother's whereabouts.

ENVIRONMENTAL FACTORS

Demographic Factors

Mr. Smith possesses several demographic risk factors that are associated with completed suicide. He is a single, white, unemployed male with psychiatric diagnoses and a history of substance abuse. These factors place Mr. Smith at greater risk for suicide than people who do not have this demographic profile. On the other hand, demographic factors that militate against suicide are his young age, good health and the lack of severe psychiatric disorders such as depression that are associated with completed suicide.

Life Events and Life Circumstances

Mr. Smith is currently under a good deal of emotional stress. His immediate concerns appear to be triggered by wanting to be placed in a hospital rather than remaining in jail, but that is exacerbated by the potential loss of his relationship with his girlfriend and the loss of his freedom if he receives another prison sentence. In response to direct questions about whether he was going to commit suicide, he said that if he were not moved to the hospital, he would kill himself.

Support Systems

It appears that Mr. Smith has very limited support systems, both in his community and in his personal life. While he is familiar with how to get assistance from social service agencies, if he were returned to the community in the near future, the immediate availability of those services would be in question. However, it seems ironic that he has access to a wide range of support services in his present situation. In fact, a case can be made that Mr. Smith has better access to sources of social and emotional support while he remains in the criminal justice system than if he were released back into the community. In terms of his family, his support system is nonexistent. His mother is not part of his life and he has no siblings. Based on his information, he doesn't have many friends and none that actually act as positive support. He does have a girlfriend, but from what he reports, they have a difficult relationship that often causes problems instead of serving to ame-liorate them. In the end, he doesn't seem to have any source of real personal support and in terms of community support, while it is available to him, it is irrelevant unless he uses it.

LETHALITY

Intent to Die

When questioned directly about his current desire to die, Mr. Smith said that he really does not want to die, but he also does not want to say where he is. He said that if he has to cut himself to be transferred to a hospital, that is the price he will pay and if that results in his death, "so be it." "If you don't think I will kill myself," he added, "just leave me here and see what happens. I warned you, now it's on you."

Based on Mr. Smith's statements during the interview, it does not appear that he is currently motivated to die. Mr. Smith has a long history of threatening suicide or engaging in sui-cide-like acts to manipulate his environment. However, these acts have not been intended to bring about his death. At times they have caused physical injury and when the injuries were serious, it was most likely a result of miscalculation or impul-siveness. His current suicide threats fall into the same cate-gory. They reflect misdirected anger and an attempt to obtain secondary gain, but they do not suggest that he currently wants to die.

Suicide Plan

Because he repeatedly made statements about killing himself, I asked Mr. Smith on several occasions if he had thought about any specific ways he might commit suicide. He initial-ly responded by saying he would cut himself using a razor blade or piece of glass. When questioned further, he went on to say that he might hang himself with his sheets, run his head into the wall or drink cleaning supplies. He told me there are many ways to kill yourself and when he decided to do it, no one could stop him. Although Mr. Smith's statements are true, they do not reflect the development of an organized, well-formulated plan to commit suicide at this time. Rather, it appears that any actions he might take in the near future would be spontaneous and opportunistic rather than calculated. His history suggests that any future suicidal episode might involve cutting himself or ingesting a medication or substance. This would also be consistent with his current level of knowledge and access to a means of death.

Access to and Knowledge of Means

In his present situation, Mr. Smith does not have access to any highly lethal means of death such as firearms. Because he is currently confined, he has very limited access to the most lethal means of committing suicide, but there are a few things that are available to him, including sheets, sharp objects and cleaning chemicals. It also does not appear that he has made an effort to obtain any means to commit suicide while he has been in jail. This, of course, does not mean that he could not commit suicide even under these conditions, particularly because he has been able to cut himself in the past and that data show that most suicides in custody occur by hanging. However, his current status severely restricts his access to most lethal means of death that would be available to him if he were in the community.

Based on what Mr. Smith said during the interview, it does not appear that he has made any overt attempts to increase his knowledge about ways to commit suicide. He did talk about knowing someone in prison who committed suicide by hanging himself, but this information appeared to be acquired casually rather than purposefully. In most of his previous self-destructive episodes, he cut himself on the wrist or forearm. It appears that he has not only learned that his method attracts attention, but also that it is not likely to kill him. On two occasions, he claims to have impulsively taken available medications, but even if true, he said he had no knowledge about the medications' lethal properties. He also has not used this method for some time, choosing instead to cut himself in each of his last three episodes. He said that the last time he cut himself was much more serious and potentially life-threatening than previous acts, but this was not supported by the available treatment record and did not seem to reflect a deliberate effort to commit an extremely lethal act.

PSYCHOLOGICAL FACTORS

Psychiatric Disorders

Mr. Smith's comments and behavior during the interview indicate that he is an individual who has difficulty relating to others. He reported numerous instances of extremely unstable interpersonal relationships which, after a brief period of time, almost always ended in conflict and turmoil. In most of these instances, it appears that the conflicts were triggered by Mr. Smith's intense overreactions to relatively moderate disagreements or differences in opinion. Judging from the available reports, this interactional style has been highly consistent over the years, showing a relatively unchanging pattern of behavior extending back to early adolescence.

Mr. Smith also described many occasions when he engaged in dangerous, self-defeating behavior that harmed both himself and others. He frequently drove while intoxicated, engaged in unprotected sex with many partners, used unclean needles and has been in many fights, sometimes requiring him or others to seek medical treatment. When I questioned him about these situations, I found that his behavior was usually a spontaneous reaction to some external event that he impulsively initiated with little regard for the long-term consequences of his actions. Law enforcement records verify some of his statements, indicating that he has been in prison and has been arrested many times for driving while intoxicated, drug possession, assault and battery and vagrancy. His probation and parole treatment records from outpatient drug treatment programs also show that he has a long history of drug and alcohol abuse and has engaged in numerous threats and acts of self-injury.

Mr. Smith exhibited a number of behaviors commonly associated with personality disorders. In fact, his most recent treatment records indicated that since the age of 8 he has been in psychiatric hospitals and correctional and social service facilities, where he periodically received diagnoses of this type. Over the last 14 years, he has been diagnosed with Adjustment Disorder, Disturbance of Conduct, Dependent Personality Disorder and Antisocial Personality Disorder. The most recent diagnosis was received 3 months ago when Mr. Smith was taken to the Woodridge Hospital emergency room by Officer Donald Wright of the Woodridge Police Department after he cut his wrist while arguing with his girlfriend. At that time he was diagnosed with Borderline Personality Disorder.

Suicidal Ideation

During the interview, Mr. Smith made numerous statements about killing himself. However, when I asked him specific questions about why he wanted to commit suicide, Mr. Smith could offer no reason for wanting to die other than that his immediate demands were not being met. Mr. Smith also said that he often thinks about suicide. Questions about these thoughts revealed that Mr. Smith often entertains fantasies about dying as a first-line coping strategy to help him deal with frustrating life situations, but he does not spend time engaging in serious planning to end his life.

Mr. Smith said that he typically takes life one day at a time, having very little in the way of a long-term life plan. He did express a fairly pessimistic view of his future, particularly about his ability to stop drinking and stay out of jail. However, after direct questioning, he did not voice any specific plans or strong desires to change any of these things. Although he clearly understands the self-defeating nature of his current behavior, Mr. Smith appeared resigned to his present lifestyle. He stated "this is the way things always have been and they will probably stay that way in the future." While the relationship he has with his current girlfriend seems very unstable, he expects the relationship to continue and expresses a strong desire to return to her after he is released.

Cognitive Style

Mr. Smith's thinking is dominated by his impulsive, poorly organized style of thought processing. He is reactive rather than contemplative and responds to most life events emotionally without thinking through the implications of his actions. He is an unimaginative and inflexible problem-solver, finding it difficult to develop alternative methods to cope with even simple problems once his initial strategy has failed. He does not, however, internalize his failures. Rather, he blames his difficulties on others and then strikes out in anger against those he sees as the source of his frustration. Consequently, he feels little guilt about how his actions affect other people or responsibility for understanding their values or motives.

EVALUATION OF RISK POTENTIAL

It should be noted that precise prediction of suicide and other self-injurious behavior is difficult and of limited reliability. Furthermore, it has been shown that the accuracy of all predictions diminishes significantly over time. However, based on the information available at the time of this assessment, Mr. Smith's current probability of suicide is considered to be LOW. This level of risk will change over time and should be modified as Mr. Smith's circumstances change. Of primary concern is the appearance of additional risk factors such as signs of depression, more pessimistic thinking about his future or an increase in his suicidal preoccupation. Mr. Smith should be monitored to ensure he is not developing a lethal suicide plan or an increased intent to die. Use of alcohol should be considered a significant risk-escalating factor as well as any further breakdown of his already fragile social support system.

TREATMENT RECOMMENDATIONS

Mr. Smith is a 28-year-old Caucasian male who was referred by authorities from the county jail after threatening to commit suicide. The results of Mr. Smith's assessment indicate he is currently a low risk for suicide. He does possess some risk factors associated with completed suicide, including several demographic variables, many past episodes of self-destructive behavior, psychiatric diagnoses, substance abuse and current emotional distress. He also exhibits an ineffective approach to interpersonal problem-solving and has limited support systems. All of these risk factors increase his potential for suicide.

On the other hand, Mr. Smith's psychiatric diagnoses are not indicative of severe mental illness or a depressive disorder. He does not express, nor do his actions indicate, a strong desire to die and he has no organized suicide plan. Of significance is the fact that Mr. Smith has made many suicide threats and engaged in a large number of self-injurious behaviors, some of which have resulted in physical injury. Although the potential seriousness of these actions cannot be ignored, it must be emphasized that they were intended to exert control over his environment and not to cause his death. Given his history, it is likely that he will continue to engage in these acts in the future. Each of these episodes, if they occur, must be closely evaluated for their intent to bring about death and must be responded to accordingly.

To respond to Mr. Smith appropriately, it will be critical to accurately identify the motivation for his acts. Nonlethal acts engaged in for purposes of manipulation should be managed by ensuring that the potential for serious physical injury is minimized, while more lethally motivated acts should focus on the psychological factors that lead to the act. In either case, taking steps to avoid permanent injury or accidental death will be important. In his present situation, Mr. Smith has a reliable and readily available social support system that he probably won't have if he is released into the community. However, the benefits of these services will depend on Mr. Smith's willingness to use them. At this point, Mr. Smith is not suicidal and his low suicide risk does not warrant hospital admission to prevent him from committing suicide. Mr. Smith should be followed to assess any changes in his suicide risk status.

Sample Risk Assessment Report: A High-Risk Example

BASIC INFORMATION

Robert Jones is a 73-year-old Caucasian male who was referred for evaluation by John Jackson, MD, attending physician at Tri-County Convalescent Center. Mr. Jones is a chronic care patient at Tri-County who has a long and complicated medical history. On April 1, 1999, I interviewed Mr. Jones in his room in the convalescent center. I never met Mr. Jones prior to this interview, which lasted approximately 1 hour.

REASON FOR ASSESSMENT

Mr. Jones was referred after nursing staff at Tri-County discovered a large quantity of pills, wrapped in cellophane, hidden under his mattress. Examination of the pills indicated they were Darvon N, a pain medication that Mr. Jones is given twice a day by the nursing staff at the center. Dr. Jackson's referral letter indicates that Mr. Jones has been exhibiting increasing signs of depression since suffering a stroke approximately 7 months ago. The stroke left him with only limited use of his left arm and leg. According to Dr. Jackson, since the stroke, Mr. Jones has expressed feelings of hopelessness and despair. He has also been quieter and withdrawn and has decreased his involvement in ward activities. Dr. Jackson began treating him for depression with medication on October 12, 1998, but after the discovery of the pills, Dr. Jackson is now concerned that Mr. Jones' state of depression has increased significantly to the point that he may be planning to take his own life. Dr. Jackson referred him for evaluation to determine if he is currently suicidal.

SOURCES OF INFORMATION

I had an opportunity to review Mr. Jones' full medical record prior to the interview. The record was very complete and did not indicate that Mr. Jones had any prior history of suicide, psychiatric illness, or mental health treatment.

PHYSICAL APPEARANCE AND BEHAVIORAL OBSERVATIONS

When I arrived for the interview, Mr. Jones was lying on his bed. His television was on but he was obviously not paying attention to the program. He appeared to be immersed in thought and disengaged from his surroundings. Even though it was a bright and sunny day, the shades were drawn and the room was dark, creating a somewhat somber atmosphere. Mr. Jones, wearing a hospital gown, was clean but appeared somewhat unkempt and disorganized, even for someone who was bedridden. When I introduced myself, Mr. Jones acknowledged that he had talked to Dr. Jackson and knew I was coming. He offered me a seat near his bed, shook my hand and asked me what I needed to know. His behavior gave the impression that he was a reserved, "no-nonsense" individual who was trying to be courteous, but simply did not choose to waste time with unnecessary niceties.

Although he was polite and cooperative, Mr. Smith sometimes seemed minimally engaged in the conversation, as if he was preoccupied with more important matters. Periodically he wandered from the topic, required things to be repeated, and responded minimally to inquiries. When this occurred, he seemed genuinely embarrassed and apologized, but within a short period it would happen again. Most of the time he spoke in a low monotone voice and exhibited a very limited range of emotions. Although this behavior was fairly characteristic of his interactions, it was more noticeable in the early stages of the interview. As time when on and we began to discuss more personal matters, his responses became more forthcoming, his attention increased and his overall engagement with the process improved.

The background information he provided was consistent with the hospital records and was complete in every detail. The quality and detail of his descriptions suggested that Mr. Jones' poor concentration during the interview could probably be attributed to psychological factors rather than to cognitive deficits or medical complications.

Although a man of few words, Mr. Jones was quite capable of making his feelings and ideas understood. His style was candid, open and to the point. In fact, he presented things in such a dispassionate, detached manner that it was almost as if he was talking about someone else. This was the case whether he was talking about objective material or deeply emotional matters. His frankness was obvious when I asked him why he was saving his doses of medication. He looked straight into my eyes and said very matter-of-factly, "Why do you think? I was going to kill myself with them." He went on to say, "My only mistake was that I waited too long and they found them. I'll get another chance. I'll make it next time."

HISTORICAL FACTORS

Personal History

Mr. Jones reported no previous contacts with mental health professionals. He said he was blessed with very good health and was never hospitalized before. Shortly after his wife died, his children tried to encourage him to see a psychiatrist, but he never did. He said he didn't believe in "that sort of thing." As he put it, "people have to learn to take care of themselves." When asked about his willingness to become involved in counseling, he said he wasn't particularly keen on the idea but that he might consider it. He also said he would continue to take his antidepressant medication, hastening to add, "but it probably won't make me feel better or change my mind [about suicide]."

Mr. Jones has never attempted suicide. However, following his wife's death, he admitted to purchasing a gun for the purpose of killing himself. He did not follow through with his plans because one of his children was hospitalized and he had to help the family by caring for his grandchildren. After the family crisis was resolved, he said he no longer felt as depressed and began doing volunteer work in the community. He said that this took his mind off his troubles. After that, he said he never really thought much about killing himself again until he realized he would never be able to leave the hospital.

Family History

Mr. Jones reports that he is one of two children, but his older brother, Ralph, committed suicide approximately 10 years ago. Hospital records confirm that his brother was diagnosed with multiple sclerosis years earlier and became progressively more incapacitated over a 15-year period. Finally, after he became almost totally disabled, he shot himself to death one night while his family was asleep. When Mr. Jones was questioned about the death, he said that he and his brother were not very close, but that he looked up to him when he was younger. He remembers one person at the funeral saying that maybe his brother's death was for the best because he was now at peace and was no longer a burden to his family. Mr. Jones said that initially he was angered by the statement and didn't understand how anyone could say that. Now he says that he not only understands the sentiment, but agrees with it.

His father died when Mr. Jones was 11 years old and his mother had trouble living a normal life without him. When Mr. Jones was a teenager, his mother was diagnosed with depression and for many years after, she was on medication and in counseling. His brother left home at an early age, leaving Mr. Jones alone at home with his mother. He reports that while he was growing up, she was so quiet and kept so much to herself that he didn't feel particularly close to her. Mr. Jones left home at the age of 17 to join the army and fight in World War II. His mother died while he was overseas and he was unable to return home for the funeral. He said that he knows there was nothing he could do about it, but he has always felt guilty about not being able to get home for the funeral.

ENVIRONMENTAL FACTORS

Demographic Factors

Mr. Jones possesses virtually all of the demographic risk factors associated with suicidality. He is an elderly, widowed, white male who has a serious medical illness. He has a psychiatric diagnosis and is not employed. Although these factors are not, in and of themselves, clear predictors of suicide, the large number of factors present in Mr. Jones' case clearly places him in the high-risk demographic group.

Life Events and Life Circumstances

Mr. Jones is currently experiencing a good deal of emotional stress and discomfort mainly because of his physical incapacitation. He seems particularly concerned by the loss of independence the stroke has caused and the potential impact that will have on his family. However, it also appears he has not satisfactorily resolved many issues relating to the loss of his wife, and the combination of being alone and disabled has been an overwhelming blow to his ability to cope. At this point, he sees no way to change his present life situation and views this as a totally unacceptable way to live. In response to several direct questions, Mr. Jones made it very clear that he thinks he would be better off dead than living like this forever.

Support Systems

Not only is Mr. Jones' wife deceased, but based on his description of his existing support systems, it appears that he has few friends and only limited support from his children. Mr. Jones has two adult children who have families of their own and do not have regular contact with him. Moreover, Mr. Jones has said that he does not feel it is his children's responsibility to care for him and would not ask them for help. Aside from the resources at the convalescent center, it does not appear that Mr. Jones has any viable support mechanisms available to him now or in the foreseeable future.

LETHALITY

Intent to Die

When directly questioned about his current feelings about suicide, Mr. Jones made it very clear that he wants to die. The circumstances surrounding the current referral also leave room for no other conclusion than that Mr. Jones was motivated solely by a desire to die. There were no manipulative qualities to his behavior in that he made no conditions contingent on his actions. In fact, he made no effort, even subtly, to let anyone know that he was contemplating suicide. He also does not evidence any ambivalence about dying. Mr. Jones chose the most lethal method available to him and endured considerable physical pain to accumulate the needed amount of medication. It appears the only reason his suicide was not completed was the completely unforeseen discovery of the pills before he could take them. Every aspect of Mr. Jones' conversation and actions suggests he possesses a very strong desire to die and is motivated to commit suicide.

Suicide Plan

When I asked Mr. Jones how he had managed to get such a large quantity of medication, he said that it had been relatively easy because no one was expecting him to attempt suicide. As a result, the nurses didn't watch him very closely when he took his pills. He said that he had begun complaining about increased pain for several weeks and eventually he was able to convince one of the doctors to increase his level of medication. When he was given his medication, he would put it under his tongue and spit it out after the nurses left the room. He only took what medication he needed to keep his pain tolerable and asked for increases every time he saw a doctor. He said that the nurse who usually took care of him in the early morning often had to cover several wards and she was therefore away from his floor for hours at a time. Whenever his nurse had to leave, she would come in and tell him that if he needed anything, he should call another nurse or another nursing station. He said that when he had accumulated enough pills, he was going to wait until the nurse on the early shift left the floor and then take the medication. He estimated that he would be dead before she returned.

When Mr. Jones was asked what he planned to do now that his medication had been taken, he said that he did not know. He did say, however, that he would think of something. Based on his statements, it does not appear that Mr. Jones has formulated an alternative plan to commit suicide at this time. His previous plan, on the other hand, was very well-organized and required considerable motivation and planning to execute. It required Mr. Jones to increase his level of knowledge about his medications, to endure significant pain to stockpile his medications and to arrange the timing of the attempt to coincide with the least likelihood of being discovered. Although he currently may not have such an elaborately designed plan for a future attempt, he clearly has the desire and ability to construct such a plan. This should be taken into account when monitoring Mr. Jones in the future.

Access to and Knowledge of Means

Mr. Jones currently has very limited access to any highly lethal means of death other than his medication. He should be monitored very closely and any activities, such as visits and outings on the ward, should be intensely supervised to ensure that he does not use the opportunity to obtain the means to kill himself. His behavior in his room should also be observed to ensure that he does not attempt to use his bedding or sharp objects such as razor blades, knives or broken glass to commit suicide.

Mr. Jones said he had given serious thought to how he might kill himself following his wife's death. After considerable deliberation, he eventually decided on shooting himself because it offered the greatest likelihood of being successful. He said that he was totally unprepared for his stroke and once he was hospitalized, he had no way of obtaining his gun. After some months, he realized that he would never be able to get back home to get his gun, and therefore he began to talk with nursing staff about his medications. After many conversations with different nurses, he was able to determine that his pain medication was the most lethal medication he could obtain and he began saving his doses. At one point, he even concocted a story about having a reaction to his medication in order to convince a volunteer to bring him a book on prescription medications from the library so he could determine how many pills he would need to take.

PSYCHOLOGICAL FACTORS

Psychiatric Disorders

Mr. Jones said that he has been thinking about killing himself for some time. His recent stroke was a major factor in his decision to do it now because the stroke has left him incapacitated to the point that he must now rely on others. However, his depression began 2 years ago when his wife of 48 years died suddenly from a heart attack. Initially he found it hard to live without her and repeatedly thought about suicide, on one occasion going so far as to buy a gun and bullets. He said that he had trouble sleeping, had little or no appetite, and did not have the energy to do much of anything during the day. He withdrew from most of the activities that he and his wife had done together "because they were no fun any-

more without her." He had trouble thinking and concentrating and would find himself walking around the house aim-
lessly for hours at a time, crying, feeling empty inside and
unneeded. He said these feelings persisted for many months
before things began to turn around. However, even today he
often thinks about his wife and still cannot believe she is
gone. After 6 months, he began to spend time in his garden
and became a volunteer at the YMCA, coaching youth sports.
He also visited his children several times and traveled in
Europe for 3 months.

It was shortly after his return to the United States that Mr.
Jones had a severe stroke. He has been hospitalized since
April of this year with little chance to be able to live indepen-
dently again. He said that at first he was only worried about
staying alive. But as time went on and he realized exactly how
dependent he would be on others, he again started to become
depressed. He said that he feels worse now than when his
wife died. At least then, he had his health and some independence; now he has nothing. At one point he said, "I have
absolutely no reason to live. I am nothing more than a burden
to everyone...including myself." Based on notes in the medical record and on Mr. Jones' own statements, he appears to
exhibit a number of symptoms associated with a mood disorder, specifically a Major Depressive Disorder. His current
symptoms are directly related to his medical condition, which
has left him permanently disabled, but it also appears that he
experienced significant depression after his wife's death. It
was not treated at the time.

Suicidal Ideation

Mr. Jones made numerous direct references about committing suicide during the interview. It was very clear from his
conversation that he desired to die and that he had given the

subject a good deal of serious thought. He seemed preoccupied with planning his death and admitted to spending hours thinking about why suicide was the best solution to his problems and how he would go about it. Mr. Jones' comments also suggest that he has a very negative future orientation in terms of life plans and expectations. Mr. Jones has cut himself off from any activities with his children, friends and even other patients. He is very pessimistic and negative about his current life situation and repeatedly said that he can see no way to change his situation in the foreseeable future. Finally, he said he feels ineffective and useless because the stroke has robbed him of his independence. This seems to greatly affect his self-perception, which has always been based on being self-sufficient and self-reliant.

Cognitive Style

The most salient aspect of Mr. Jones' thinking is his conspicuous inability to focus on anything other than the negative consequences of his current situation. His thinking is very rigid and constricted, making him unable to see any positive alternatives to his problems other than suicide. Because he now sees suicide as the only possible solution to his problems, he refuses to explore other options. Mr. Jones' level of pessimism combined with his cognitive rigidity makes it extremely difficult for him to develop constructive methods of coping with his situation.

EVALUATION OF RISK POTENTIAL

It should be noted that precise prediction of suicide and other self-injurious behavior is difficult and of limited reliability. Furthermore, it has been shown that the accuracy of all predictions diminishes significantly over time. However, based on the information available at the time of this assessment,

Mr. Jones' current probability of suicide is considered to be EXTREME. Because his chances of making a serious and highly lethal attempt in the near future are highly possible, immediate precautions to avoid his suicide should be implemented. This ultimate level of risk may change over time and it should be modified as Mr. Jones' circumstances change.

TREATMENT RECOMMENDATIONS

Mr. Jones is 73-year-old Caucasian male who was referred by his attending physician to assess his potential for committing suicide. The results of Mr. Jones' assessment indicate that he currently represents an extreme risk for suicide. He possesses a very large number of risk factors for suicide that significantly increases the likelihood that he will make an attempt in the near future if adequate interventions are not implemented. Mr. Jones should be monitored very closely and followed regularly to determine if his level of suicidality changes. He should also be observed very closely to ensure that he does not have an opportunity to make a suicide attempt. Mr. Jones could benefit from formal counseling, antidepressant medication, and efforts to engage him in activities with people in his surroundings.

Index

About the Author

Thomas W. White received his Ph.D. in clinical psychology from the University of Kansas. As an intern at the Menninger Foundation in Topeka, Kansas, he worked in the Law and Psychiatry Program at the Center for Applied Behavioral Sciences. He pursued his forensic interests at the Federal Bureau of Prisons, where, for 15 years, he was Chief Psychologist, providing direct clinical services for several different federal correctional facilities. For the last 10 years, Dr. White has been Regional Administrator for Psychology Services at the Federal Bureau of Prisons.

In addition to his career in public service, Dr. White has made contributions to the professional psychology community through teaching, lecturing and writing. For over 21 years, Dr. White has taught both graduate and undergraduate courses. He has authored and co-authored chapters in numerous books and he has also written articles for psychology and correctional publications. Dr. White is past Chair of the Criminal Justice Section of Division 18 of the American Psychological Association and is affiliated with several other professional organizations.

After years as a psychologist in private practice, Dr. White is now actively involved in training and consulting activities. He regularly conducts training seminars on a variety of topics in both the public and private sector. He provides technical assistance in suicide prevention and policy development internationally and offers workshops in suicide assessment to a wide variety of local, state and federal agencies.

Readers of this book are encouraged to contact Dr. White with comments or questions about the H.E.L.P.E.R. system. Inquiries about Dr. White's availability for conducting training seminars in suicide assessment should be sent to the address below.

Training and Consulting Services
Post Office Box 17146
Kansas City, KS 66117
Phone: 913-683-5321
E-mail: HELPER_SYSTEM@yahoo.com